Sword & Spirit

Tengu, from a mid-Edo period Jigen-ryu scroll.
Tom Dreitlein Collection.

Sword
& Spirit

Classical Warrior
Traditions of Japan
Volume Two

Edited by
Diane Skoss

Koryu Books
Berkeley Heights, New Jersey

Published by Koryu Books
P.O. Box 86
Berkeley Heights, NJ 07922-0086
e-mail: ss2@koryubooks.com
http://www.koryubooks.com/books/ss2.html
fax: 1-212-208-4366; toll-free tel: 1-888-665-6798
First printed 1999
Book and cover design by Koryu Books
Printed in the United States of America

Photo and illustration credits:
Cover photo of Kanzaki Masaru demonstrating Shojitsu Kenri Kataichi-ryu at the
   Nippon Budokan ©1997 Inoue Kazuhiro.
Frontispiece courtesy Tom Dreitlein.
Reproduction of "Takeda Clan Samurai" by Obata Chiura on page 45, courtesy
   Richard & Kimi Hill.
Photos on pages 62, 66, 77, 82, 83, 85, 86, 98, 99 ©1997 Inoue Kazuhiro;
   page 74 ©1995 Inoue Kazuhiro. Used with the permission of the photographer.
Photo on page 69 ©1997 Ron Beaubien. Used with permission.
Photo on page 80 ©1997 Michael Ashworth. Used with permission.
Photos on pages 131, 138, 139, 142, 143 ©1998 Liam Keeley. Used with permission.
Calligraphy on page 133 ©1998 Hirato Hiroko. Used with permission.
Photo on page 174 ©1995 Joe Cieslik. Used with permission.
All other photos are from the collection of Meik and Diane Skoss.
"Kabala in Motion: Kata & Pattern Practice in the Traditional Bugei" by Karl Friday
   was previously published in the *Journal of Asian Martial Arts* (1995 4:4).
   Reproduced with permission of author and publisher.

Publisher's Cataloging-in-Publication
(Provided by Quality Books, Inc.)

Sword & spirit /edited by Diane Skoss. -- 1st ed.
      p. cm. -- (Classical warrior traditions of Japan ; 2)
      Includes bibliographical references and index.
      LCCN: 98-85052
      ISBN: 1-890536-05-9

      1. Martial arts--Japan.   I. Skoss, Diane.
   II. Title: Sword and spirit

GV1100.77.A2S96 1999   796.86'0952
                               QBI98-1444

To my teachers:

Wakimoto Yasuharu

Phil Relnick

Nitta Suzuyo

Note on the Japanese in this text: Combine specialized terminology with a foreign language not written in the roman alphabet and you get quite a tangle. We have tried to establish and follow consistent guidelines; these are outlined in the "Koryu Books Japanese Style Sheet" (available at ftp.koryubooks.com as stylesheet.txt). Japanese names are given in Japanese order, surname first, except where the individual is a long-term resident of the West or is writing in English. Japanese terms (i.e. ones not found in *Webster's Third International Dictionary*) are presented in italics the first time they appear in each essay. Transliteration is based on a modified Hepburn system and long vowels are not specially marked. Japanese terms are translated where necessary in the text and translations are also provided in the index. Citations generally follow the *Chicago Manual of Style's* "author/date" system; parenthetical page numbers (with author and date where necessary) refer to items listed in the "Reference" section at the end of each chapter.

CONTENTS

FOREWORD

I would like to extend my very heartfelt congratulations to Diane Skoss, wife of my long-time student, Meik Skoss, on the founding of her new publishing company, Koryu Books. These two intend to publish books in English to introduce the traditional Japanese martial arts to a Western audience.

Meik Skoss came to Japan in the 1970s. After training in aikido for several years in Shingu, Wakayama Prefecture, he moved to Tokyo and entered my dojo there, to begin his study of Yagyu Shinkage-ryu. He has been a very earnest, diligent student and is a valued member of the ryu. He has studied a wide variety of modern and classical martial arts, including Tendo-ryu naginatajutsu (under Sawada Hanae Sensei). Under Nitta Suzuyo Sensei both he and his wife have learned the highest levels of Toda-ha Buko-ryu naginatajutsu; together they have presented excellent exhibitions at demonstrations of the classical martial arts throughout Japan.

This upcoming volume is a continuation of the work of the pioneer foreign researcher on the Japanese classical martial arts, Donn Draeger. Naturally, I am very pleased that two of my own students, David Hall [who contributed to volume one, *Koryu Bujutsu*] and Meik Skoss, American researchers who are continuing Draeger's work, have persevered in their study and training and have been able to contribute to this series. I am sure that this book, and future volumes as well, will be invaluable to people outside of Japan who are studying the Japanese classical martial arts; I sincerely hope that it is read by many.

Yagyu Nobuharu
21st headmaster, Yagyu Shinkage-ryu hyoho

Yagyu Nobuharu is a direct descendant of the founder of the school, Yagyu Sekishusai Munetoshi, and he is the first member of his family to have pursued a profession in addition to teaching swordsmanship. He now teaches and lectures on the principles of the Yagyu Shinkage-ryu and serves as a standing director of the two major classical martial arts organizations in Japan, the Nihon Kobudo Shinkokai and the Nihon Kobudo Kyokai.

PREFACE

The Japanese *furoshiki*, a simple square of sturdy, decorative cloth, is an elegant and ingenious solution to all sorts of packing dilemmas. It can be used in place of a shopping bag, as a small spare suitcase, or as an organizer. Many martial artists in Japan (and elsewhere) still wrap their training wear, neatly folded, in one of these modest versatile cloths. There's no need to arrange the content to conform to the container — the furoshiki adapts to any shape.

Sword & Spirit is a little like a furoshiki. The chapters herein do not all stack up precisely and neatly into one uniform package. Some are solid and hard-edged, others more reflective. Individually they present widely various topics woven together by the woof and warp of the Japanese warrior traditions. There is history, both of the ancient Warring States period, and the more recent events of World War II; there are insights into Japanese social structures, etiquette, human combative behavior; and there is close analysis of techniques of Japanese classical swordsmanship. Each chapter is offered as a uniquely shaped source, uninterpreted so that you can unwrap the meanings that are of most use to you now.

My goal has been to provide something for everyone — the passionately involved, those who are just curious, the explorer, the newcomer, the historian, the student of social history. I hope too that this volume will be something you can return to again in the future, when it will have new messages to reveal. Initial reports from readers of the first volume, *Koryu Bujutsu*, are encouraging — each chapter has its fans, and different people are discovering entirely different lessons within its pages.

None of this would be possible, of course, without the contributors who have so generously shared their insights and knowledge. My deepest thanks to each of them. Also my most sincere gratitude to the many others who have helped to make this book possible in various ways — translators Derek Steel and Yoko Sato; copy editor extraordinaire

SWORD & SPIRIT

Richard Florence; and photographers Inoue Kazuhiro, Ron Beaubien, Mike Ashworth. Tom Dreitlein, Richard Hill, and Joe Cieslik kindly helped to provide very special illustrations. Steve Duncan has been invaluable as both sympathetic "ear" and in managing the Koryu Books warehouse during these early transitional years. Steve Kelsey, Andy Nordgren (my brother), Ellis Amdur, G. Cameron Hurst III, and Mark Wiley were kind enough to take time to read an early version of the manuscript, and members of the Publishers Marketing Association e-mail list answered questions, wrote software, and provided book business advice. Thank you one and all!

Finally, I'd like to dedicate this book to Wakimoto Yasuharu, my jukendo teacher, who along with my husband Meik Skoss got me well and truly started along the "way"; and to Phil Relnick and Nitta Suzuyo, my teachers in the classical traditions. Without these exemplars, I would never have known of the rich beauty of the koryu.

Diane Skoss

Diane Skoss began her martial arts training in 1982 while at Indiana University finishing up master's degrees in library science and English literature. In 1987 she moved to Japan to further her study of aikido; it was during her ten-year stay in Tokyo that she met and trained with the teachers who inspired this book. She holds the license of okuden in Toda-ha Buko-ryu naginatajutsu, and has dan grades in jukendo, aikido, jodo, and tankendo. Her publishing career began modestly as an editor for **Aiki News/Aikido Journal***; soon she was managing that publication and was responsible for book production as well. In 1996 she started her own publishing company devoted to the classical Japanese martial arts; this is its second production.*

Dave Lowry is the author of a number of books on the Japanese martial arts; his most recent is **Persimmon Wind** *(1998). His articles and columns appear in a number of magazines, including* **Furyu: The Budo Journal**. *He began training in the classical Japanese arts in 1968, and is one of those exceedingly rare individuals to have done most of his training in the classical traditions outside of Japan.*

INTRODUCTION
A COCONUT PALM IN MISSOURI

Dave Lowry

If you want to understand the difficulties in introducing to the West something like the *koryu bujutsu*, the classical martial disciplines of old Japan, begin by imagining a coconut.

Think of the whole tree, the curving trunk, waving fronds, hanging clusters of nuts, thriving happily on the sandy shore of some Polynesian island. Then imagine that same tree hoisted up, roots and all, and transported to the front lawn of a suburban home. In America's Midwest. In February. Now you've got the picture.

This analogy was a favorite of my sensei, a man who knows little about South Pacific flora and who learned more than he wanted to know about Februarys in Missouri during his years of living there, but who knows a great deal about the bujutsu of Japan. These arts, he suggested, when they are transported into the alien culture of the modern world, face almost precisely the same perils as that tropical coconut transplanted so rudely into a frosty yard in Missouri. Like the tree, they are deprived of the soil in which they germinated and grew. They are bereft of a specific climate to which they have been uniquely adapted over a long, long period of time. And most importantly, both the koryu and the coconut have been dropped into an environment that is, at best indifferent to their survival; at worst it is openly hostile.

I met Diane Skoss, this book's editor, in the mid-summer of 1998. We were attending a *gasshuku*, a kind of training camp/slumber party/road trip, for one of the few koryu actively practiced and taught outside Japan. Driving through the lush green hills of central Ohio every morning and evening back and forth to the training site, we had long discussions about the difficulties of the koryu transplanted into the West. We are both practitioners; moreover, we both write about the bujutsu and so our interests are proprietary as well as academic and professional. And so we had a lot to talk about.

I don't know that we came to any great conclusions that summer. We were, in fact, left with more questions than answers. How well may we realistically expect any art to survive in an environment and society completely alien? Should we even try? Suppose that we do: might we end up with some kind of weird hybrid? And will these arts, even if they survive that first long winter of transplantation, ever be capable of staying healthy enough to successfully reproduce into future generations?

It's not that Diane and other Western koryu exponents are by nature pessimists. Quite the opposite. The proof of her optimism in particular is in your hands right now. The impression I had of her was that, as it is with virtually every other non-Japanese koryu practitioner, she has an intense interest in the cultivation of these arts. She also has a kind of indomitable spirit and a sense of purpose and confidence that she can preserve and transmit the arts she has been taught. (And still continues to learn, she would hasten to have me add, I'm sure.)

Diane has spent many years in Japan, has immersed herself in its culture and become conversant in aspects of its society that are unfamiliar to even the vast majority of modern Japanese. This is, incidentally, no small feat. Living in Japan for any foreigner is challenging, frustrating, and requires some serious sacrifices. Foreigners who accomplish that and further, who manage to insinuate themselves successfully into classical or traditional arts like the bujutsu are extraordinary people. Returning to the United States and becoming busy building a life and a future here, Diane has gone to considerable effort in bringing her share of plant stock of the koryu to the West. Further, she has applied her talents as a writer and an editor to presenting these arts in an accurate and scholarly manner.

In her first book, *Koryu Bujutsu*, she assembled an impressive group of authorities who turned out an array of essays on the classical Japanese martial arts. It was the most important book — come to think of it, it was just about the *only* book — written in English on this topic since the late Donn F. Draeger's seminal writings of more than two decades earlier. This second volume presents another collection of similar essays, joined this time with contributions from a Japanese perspective, one ancient, the other contemporary. Like the first, the contents here provide a glimpse into the world of the bujutsu. The mentality necessary for learning them, the ethos which guides them, some of the history behind their creation; this is the kind of information sorely needed by those who would understand these medieval institutions. That's what this book is about. It was written entirely by individuals who know about what they write, whose facts are correct, whose knowledge has been hard- and well-earned, and whose opinions, when they venture them, should be relevant for anyone wishing to gain a grasp of the essential nature of the koryu martial arts.

In the discussions I had with Diane I was encouraged by her enthusiasm for presenting the Japanese bujutsu to Western readers. I am still not convinced the koryu can flourish in this country. Or that they can even survive at all outside of the very special environments that have been provided by the handful of experts who are trying to communicate them. They are, for all they have endured, for all their timeless strengths and values, quite fragile. They are almost instantly susceptible to the ravages of those who would deliberately seek to distort them. They may suffer even worse the blights inflicted by the well meaning who, for all their intentions, simply cannot cultivate the bujutsu because they lack a proper background and instruction. I do believe that if the classical martial arts of Japan can flower in this country and society so far from their birth and maturation, that it will be at the hands of considerate and skilled gardeners like Diane and the various authors of this book. What they have written is another important step in preparing the soil of the West for the importation of the koryu. Those who read it are bound to benefit, even if they never take up a weapon or don a *hakama*.

They will also learn something of the challenges involved in bringing coconut groves to the Midwest.

Takeda Nobushige (1525-1561) was the younger brother of the famed Takeda Shingen, warlord of Sendai, head of one of the most powerful clans in Japan during the latter part of the Warring States period (1467-1568). Nobushige, renowned as both warrior and scholar, wrote these precepts in 1558 for his eldest son as a guide to proper moral behavior. Each precept is accompanied by a relevant quotation from the Chinese classics, and the text thus served as a textbook for educating young warriors of the Takeda clan. Though the culture that engendered these "words of wisdom" is long gone, a remnant lingers in the koryu bujutsu. Substitute "headmaster" for "lord" for a surprisingly relevant guide to behavior within the Japanese ryu today. The "Ninety-Nine Precepts" were incorporated into the **Koyo Gunkan** *(see "Neglected Treasure," pages 35-57). This translation is by Alexander C. Bennett, based on the text as reproduced in Sakai Kenji's* **Koyo Gunkan Taisei** *(Tokyo: Namiko Shoin, 1995).*

KYUJUKYU KAKUN
THE NINETY-NINE PRECEPTS
OF THE TAKEDA CLAN

Takeda Nobushige

Learning is not just to enrich the body, it is also the base for the prosperity of the nation and the well-being of one's descendants. Because of this book of learning, one can recognize heaven and understand the past. How can this not be the way of sincerity? How can one know universal truth without such a book? The way will become clear with this book. Is this not a wondrous thing?[1]

1. You must not commit treachery against your lord.

It is written in the *Analects* of Confucius, "A gentleman-scholar never parts from the way of virtue no matter how preoccupied, nor does he neglect the way of virtue in times of emergency." Also, "You must serve your lord with all your heart."

2. Never be a coward in battle.

Wu-tzu[2] says, "If one clings to life, he will lose it. If one is willing to forfeit his life, he will live."

---

[1] The priest Sessan's introduction as reproduced in Sakai's *Koyo Gunkan Taisei* (1: 43).

[2] Chinese general born about 440 BC, and allegedly murdered in 361 BC. The Wade-Giles Romanization system for Chinese-Mandarin is used in this text because the terms are historical, that is, pre-People's Republic of China. The Pinyin equivalent is provided in the index.

3. Never hesitate to be courteous.

It is written in the *Shih Chi*,[3] "If the master is of good deportment, his retainers will follow him willingly. If his conduct is not good, his orders will not be obeyed."

4. One must aim to be valorous at all times.

It is written in the *San Lüeh*,[4] "Under a strong general, there will be no weak soldiers."

5. Refrain from telling lies.

In the oracle of the gods it has been said, "Honesty may not always be helpful, but in the long run it will be the best policy." In the case of strategy, however, it depends on the situation. Sun Tzu[5] says, "Even if at full military strength, avoid direct confrontation and defeat the enemy by being unpredictable."

6. Always be dutiful to your parents.

It is written in the *Analects*, "Do your best to be obedient to your parents."

7. You should not scheme in even the smallest way against your brothers.

It is written in the *Hou Han Shu*,[6] "Brothers are your left and right hands."

8. Do not speak of things outside your competence.

Yin Hang says, "A man is known by the words he utters."

---

[3] The *Shih Chi*, or *Historical Records,* is the first written dynastic history covering Chinese history from the beginning to approximately 100 BC.

[4] *The Three Briefs*, also called *Huang Shih-kung San Lüeh,* was reportedly written by T'ai Kung, author of the *Liu T'ao.*

[5] Author of *The Art of War.*

[6] *History of the Later Han Dynasty*, compiled by Fan Yeh and others in 445 AD.

9. Never be rude. Especially to priests, women, and the poor, always be polite.

It is written in the *Li Chi* (*Book of Rites*), "With courtesy, a man's life is stable; without it, dangerous."

10. Training in the warrior arts[7] *is very important.*

The *Analects* of Confucius say, "It is harmful to engage in activities outside your profession."

11. Never neglect your studies.

It is written in the *Analects*, "Learning without thinking is darkness. Thinking without study is dangerous."

12. Be familiar with the art of verse.

A poem says, "A closed heart remains concealed. Being open leads the way to greater development."

13. Pay close attention to the etiquette of ceremonies.

It is written in the *Analects* that even the master himself inquired [about the rites] at temples he visited.

14. Do not overindulge in refined pleasures.

It is written in the *Shih Chi*, "An excess of alcohol leads to disorder, an excess of joy results in misery." It is written in the *Tso Chuan*,[8] "Banquets should not be poisonous." Also it is said, "Good things are good, and virtue should be revered while lust contained."

---

[7] *Kyuba no michi* translates literally as "the way of bow and horse" but was used to refer to all aspects of the martial training of the warrior class.

[8] The *Tso Chuan* (*The Left Annals*) contains historical records of the Chinese Warring States period (403-221 BC) completed sometime during the fourth century BC.

15. Never reply rudely to a man who asks a question.

It is written in the *Analects*, "Take care not to destroy the bond of trust when associating with friends."

16. Always be patient.

It is written in the *I Ching*, "Kanshin's great feat was to persevere after the humiliation [of being raped] as a child to become a great warlord."

17. In matters both great and small, never violate the orders of your lord.

It is written in the *Analects*, "Water forms to the shape of its vessel."

18. Do not ask for fiefs or assistance from your lord.

In the *Tso Chuan* it says, "Reward without merit is unjust gain and leads to calamity."

19. Do not pass time complaining or gossiping.

An old proverb says, "If you are poor, do not flatter; if you are rich, do not be haughty."

20. It is important to be benevolent to your retainers.

It is written in the *San Lüeh*, "Your subjects are like your own hands and feet."

21. When a retainer is ill, be concerned and pay him a visit, even though this may cause some inconvenience.

It is written in the *Liu T'ao*,[9] "Tend to your men as you would to your own thirst."

[9] Also known as the *Military Pronouncements*, this text is attributed to T'ai Kung during the Warring States period.

SWORD & SPIRIT

22. Do not neglect loyal retainers.

It is written in the *San Lüeh*, "If the master cannot discern between right and wrong, retainers of merit will lose all interest."

23. You should not forgive those who slander others. However, verify such information through the use of spies and deliberate [before acting].

It is said, "If you support the good and set aside the bad, the masses will follow."

24. Be open to righteous remonstration.

The ancients said, "Good medicine is bitter tasting, but is effective treatment. Faithful words are harsh on one's ears, but improve one's conduct." It is written in the *Shang Shu*,[10] "When a piece of timber is cut along the grain it will be straight, and when a master listens to remonstrance he will be a gentleman-scholar."

25. When retainers are still loyal, but unavoidably fall into distress [and are unable to carry out their duties], their master should give them the necessary assistance.

It was said, "If you are planning to reside in a place for one year, plant the five grains. If your plans are for ten years, plant trees. If your plans are for life, there is nothing more important than sustaining your retainers."

26. Never come and go as you please through the back entrance of the master's palace.

It was said, "Father and son do not sit in the same rank, neither do men and women" [one must know one's place and make the distinction].

---

[10] *Chronicle of the Shang Dynasty* (1766-1045 BC).

27. A man who is alienated from his friends should make efforts to understand the way of humanity.

In the *Analects* it says, "Do not deviate from the way of virtue even for the time it takes to eat a meal."

28. Do not neglect everyday duties.

It was said, "If you have time and energy left after executing your duties, you should study." When attending to your duties, first go to where your peers are gathered and then retreat to the rear. It is essential to know your place. The ancients said, "After three days absence, do not expect others to be the same as they were before. This is even more so in the case of the gentleman-scholar."

29. Do not gossip in front of others, even with an intimate companion.

It was said, "Consider a matter three times before speaking of it. Consider a matter nine times before acting on it."

30. One must thoroughly study Zen meditation.

It was said, "There are no special secrets to the practice of Zen. One only needs to be aware of the importance of life and death."

31. When the master departs for home, he should send a messenger before him to announce his return. Otherwise, when he suddenly appears home, he may witness his servants' negligence and would have to scold them. Upon making a careful examination into the details of such matters, there would be no end to them.

Confucius said, "It is perverse to execute a person without first educating them [about right and wrong]."

32. A retainer should not feel disgruntled about his master's coldness toward him, no matter how unreasonable it may seem.

It is said, "The retainer must act as a retainer should even if the master does not act as a master should." It is also said that, "The person hunting a deer [in the depths of the mountain] is unable to see the mountain." Also, "A junior should not make judgements regarding a superior."

33. In punishing a retainer, if the crime is small, a scolding will suffice. If the offense is grave, the retainer must be executed.

T'ai Kung said, "Nip any evil in the bud, or you will have to use an axe." Severe punishment given on any occasion will make the retainers apprehensive. It is written in the *Lü Shih Ch'un Ch'iu*, "Too strict a rule will not be observed; too many prohibitions will not be obeyed."

34. Do not delay in presenting an award to a retainer. In rewarding a retainer, the master should be pleased whether the deed is great or small.

It is written in the *San Lüeh*, "In rewarding merit, no time is to be wasted."

35. Make an effort to confirm in detail the good or bad things that happen in your province and elsewhere.

It is said, "If you do not learn from the past, nothing will last."

36. Do not cast any extra burdens upon the peasants beyond their quota of labor.

It is written in the *Liu T'ao*, "Oppression from above causes great hardship below. If taxes are increased, crime will proliferate and people will lose all morality."

37. Never disclose rumors of mishaps in the family to outsiders.

An old proverb goes, "Good news doesn't leave the gate, but bad news travels far." It is written in the *Pi Yen Lu*, "The difficulties experienced by a house should not be discussed beyond the house."

38. When utilizing men, use them according to their abilities.

The ancients said, "A good carpenter will not cast timber aside, a good general will not abandon his men."

39. Carefully prepare your battle equipment.

The ancients said, "A nine-storied tower begins with a foundation."

40. When heading for the front, do not be even a day behind your master.

The ancients said, "A soldier should be distressed at hearing the gong [to retreat], and should be overjoyed to hear the drum [to advance]."

41. Take good care of your horse.

It is written in the *Analects*, "Dogs protect men from enemies, and horses work for men. They are to be looked after."

42. When confronting an enemy, attack the points that have not been prepared.

It is said, "The man who defeats the enemy does so by attacking unpreparedness." And, "A house with tradition will attack the enemy without giving a moment's respite."

43. Do not chase the enemy too far.

It is written in the *Ssu-ma Fa*,[11] "In chasing the enemy, do not break up the ranks. Avoiding this will save confusion in your own army, and men and horses will not be wasted."

44. If your army is winning a battle, it is advisable to continue pushing through, not giving the enemy a chance to rally. If all the enemy forces have not been destroyed, there is a danger that they will regroup.

It is written in the *San Lüeh*, "An attack should be just like the rising of the wind."

---

[11] Text dating from about the fourth century BC. The author is unknown. The title might best be translated as *The Methods of the Minister of War* or *Military Methods*.

45. At the dawn of battle, a master should treat his men harshly. By doing so, they will become enraged and fight violently against the enemy.

It is written in the *Ssu-ma Fa*, "A weak enemy should be made to obey and conform as is the nature of water. A strong vigorous enemy should be treated with the same respect and fear as fire."

46. Do not praise the enemy's strength in front of your own troops.

It is said, "Do not allow anyone to talk of the enemy's strong points."

47. Do not allow your men to defame the enemy [and thereby enrage them].

It was said, "Arouse a wasp and it will come at you with the ferocity of a dragon."

48. Do not show a weak attitude even in front of relatives or attendants.

It is written in the *San Lüeh*, "Servants and warriors will not respect a man who has lost his valor."

49. Take care not to maneuver excessively.

It was said, "Too many wishes will lead to nothing. What is to be gained from going too far from the natural course of things?" Also, "To go too far is as bad as not going far enough."

50. When intending to take the enemy by surprise, avoid the major roads and take the lesser ones.

It is said, "When you are in a position easily seen by the enemy, take the secret roads. When in a position not obvious to the enemy, attack them by the main road."

51. When asked about something, sometimes it is better to feign ignorance.

In the *Analects* it is written, "Even if it is something desirable [it can be troublesome, so] it is better to be without it."

52. A master should forget a retainer's crime if he repents after being admonished.

The *Analects* say, "Recognize the sincerity of a man who has decided to progress and learn from his past failures."

53. Although a father may be punished on account of his unpreparedness, if his sons are loyal and meritorious, they should be spared the wrath of their lord.

It was said, "The calf of a brindled ox may have red hair and fine horns. Even if you do not want to use it, do not dispose of it."

54. When deploying troops, it is necessary to discern which enemy to make peace with, which enemy to destroy, and which enemy to conquer.

It is written in the *San Lüeh*, "Strategy depends on the type of enemy."

55. A gentleman-scholar should refrain from fighting.

Confucius said, "A gentleman-scholar has nothing to fight over, but if he must, should it not be at an archery contest?"

56. Be careful to discern accurately between right and wrong.

It is written in the *San Lüeh*, "If the good deed of one is disregarded, the meritorious deeds of all will decline. If one evil deed is praised, all will revert to evil."

57. When provisions arrive at the front, the food should be divided amongst comrades-in-arms in small amounts.

It is written in the *San Lüeh*, "When there were consignments of food and wine, a great commander of old would pour the wine into the river and drink [water] with his men."

58. You cannot succeed in writing without great effort.

It is said, "Even a journey of a thousand miles begins with a single step."

59. Even if your theory is entirely reasonable, do not persist in it to a man of superior status.

There is a saying that goes, "When words are many, one's position is weakened."

60. Do not fight over a mistake. What is important is what you do after making the mistake.

Confucius said, "Never hesitate to correct an error." Also, "Making a mistake and not correcting it is the real error."

61. Even if you have carefully considered a plan, you should take heed when a contradictory opinion is offered.

It is said, "An opinion offered in good faith should be gladly accepted in good faith."

62. Do not disregard the elderly, regardless of their status.

The ancients said, "Respect the aged as you do your own parents."

63. When going to the front, finish your meal during the night, and be as alert as if you were confronting an enemy once leaving the gate until returning home.

An old saying goes, "Caution is your castle, and negligence is the enemy."

64. Refrain from associating with those of poor conduct.

In the *Shih Chi* it says, "If you do not know a man's character, consider the nature of his friends." And, "A man should not mix only with those of high status, shunning those of low station. The bush warbler that flits from blossom to blossom smells their fragrance without becoming attached to them."

65. Do not be too suspicious of others.

It is written in the *San Lüeh*, "Calamity in a great army arises only from deep mistrust."

66. Do not criticize others' mistakes.

It is said, "Bestow commendation on others."

67. Instruct retainers not to be jealous.

It is said that leaving doors unlocked invites robbers, and thick makeup incites sensuality.

68. Do not flatter.

It is written in the *Liu T'ao*, "If a man is in a high position, flattery will cause disorder and calamity among the troops."

69. Do not be late by even a moment when summoned.

It is said, "When summoned by your lord, set off without even waiting for the carriage."

70. Military secrets and spying activities should not be disclosed to others.

It is written in the *I Ching*, "Harm will result from a secret that is not kept." It is written in the *Shih Chi*, "Strategy succeeds through secrecy; [the reality reflected by] words is destroyed through divulgence."

71. Take pity on humble men.

It is written in the *Shang Shu*, "The lord's duty is to govern virtuously to protect [the well-being of] the masses."

72. Believe in the gods and Buddha.

There is a saying that goes, "One who acts in accord with the Buddha's mind will be protected, but the man who lends himself to wickedness to gain ascendancy over others will eventually fall." Also, "The gods do not help those who are disreputable."

73. *When your allies are on the verge of defeat, be roused to fight all the more.*

In the *Ku-Liang Chuan*[12] it says, "If your strategy is thoughtfully prepared, you need not fight. However, if you must fight and do it well, you will not perish."

74. *Take no notice of one who is intoxicated.*

It is written in the *Han Shu*,[13] "Once, Ping Chi, who was the secretary for the high counselor, had his carriage knocked into by a drunkard, but he did not so much as scold him."

75. *Be fairly disposed toward all.*

It is written in the *Hsiao Ching*, "Heaven and earth do not change the movement of time for the sake of one special person. The sun and the moon do not dim their light for the sake of one special person. A great lord does not change the law for the sake of one special person."

76. *Use a sharp sword, not a dull one.*

It is said that you cannot cut through bone with a dull sword.

77. *While walking around your neighborhood, be constantly aware of what is happening around you.*

Chen Fen said, "One invites disaster by being imprudent."

78. *Endeavor never to take a person's life.*

It is written in the *San Lüeh*, "The support of the people allows one to govern a state and bring peace to the families of the realm. The loss of the people results in the loss of the state and the destruction of the families of the realm."

[12] A commentary on the *Ch'un Ch'iu* reportedly written by Chi Ku-liang.

[13] *Chronicle of the Han Dynasty* (206 BC-8 AD), compiled in 92 AD by Pan Ku.

79. After retiring from your profession, avoid becoming a burden to your children.

It is written in the *Pi Yen Lu,* "Pick up your carrying pole [to take up your possessions] and conceal yourself out of the way, deep in the mountains." Also, "Refrain from trying to distinguish yourself by advancing principles of good and evil. Cease involving yourself in criticizing the evil ways of the world."

80. Do not become excessively devoted to leisure activities such as hawking, or going on excursions. Doing such things will only waste time and hamper the accomplishment of your duties.

It is said, "If you are constantly concerned with worldly troubles, you will forget the values of your family."

81. When out on an excursion, do not lose sight of yourself and others and become careless.

It is said, "When weighing something, take note of the weight of the object only, and do not give so much as a thought to the beauty of the measuring device."

82. When issuing orders to retainers during bad weather, be compassionate.

Confucius said, "A lord should avoid the busy seasons when he drafts people [for official duty]."

83. When confronting an enemy of one thousand men, attack using one hundred men from the flank.

It is said, "It is more effective for one man to unlock the gate than for one thousand men to break it."

84. Refrain from discussing battle plans indiscriminately.

An old saying goes, "Things explained based on hearsay will be mistaken." Another old proverb states, "Even a slight initial difference will be exaggerated to become as great as the gap between heaven and earth."

85. Even if you do not know the secrets of strategy necessary to win a battle, often it is advisable to pretend to know.

An old saying goes, "A man who was rumored to be as heavy as a cauldron is found to be as light as a hair."

86. Listen to what the lower classes are saying in the way of criticism but refrain from becoming angry with them. Then discreetly devise appropriate plans of action.

It was said, "Things are not always what they seem [and require careful consideration]."

87. When the master returns home from the battlefield, the retainer should reach home before his master.

It is said, "Take as much care at the end as in the beginning."

88. A man should not interfere with a colleague's affairs regardless of how close they may be.

An old saying goes, "He who dips his hand in cinnabar will be stained red, and those who touch ink will be stained black."

89. Refrain from discussing matters of food or trade in front of others.

An old saying goes, "The quality of metal is tested by fire, and that of a man by what he says."

90. Think carefully before requesting a favor, even if you are on intimate terms with someone.

The ancients said, "Being greedy for one more cup of wine, one may cause the loss of the whole boatload of fish."

91. Refrain from keeping to one group.

Confucius said, "A gentleman-scholar makes many friends and is never critical, whereas a man with a small mind is critical and makes few friends."

92. Even within a group of intimate companions, refrain from discussing indecent things. It is better to leave discreetly if the tone of the conversation turns to such.

It was said, "Determine your own mind, and vanquish the spirit of others by laughing at them."

93. Refrain from criticizing people in the presence of others.

It is written in the *Chan Kuo Ts'e*, "Speak well of another's good points; do not mention his bad ones."

94. Practice calligraphy.

An old saying goes, "The great events of the Hsia, Yin, and Chou Dynasties have been recorded for posterity thanks to the writing system."

95. In making reparations, pay a part from your own labor, and the other part from your fief. If you pay only from your fief, problems will arise.

An old saying goes, "When walking, we don't lift both feet at the same time." It is also said, "The spring sun shines evenly, but the flowers that receive the light grow to various sizes."

96. Even if the enemy's forces are many, attack if their defenses have been neglected. Moreover, be wary of attacking a small enemy if their defenses are well prepared.

Sun Tzu says, "Do not attack a well-defended camp, nor attempt to stop a well-arranged attack. To strike at such a force, keep in mind the snake of Mt. Ch'ang. When its head is struck, its tail will attack in response; and when its tail is struck, its head comes around to strike. When its body is struck, it counters with both its head and tail. There is a strategy for fighting such an enemy."

97. A virtuous warrior should not behave outlandishly.

Confucius said, "A gentleman-scholar who lacks solemnity will lose his authority."

98. *Always be alert.*

It is written in the in the *Analects*, "I reflect upon my conduct three times every day." Also, "Do not part with your sword even when in the company of your wife." It is said, "The sword that takes life, gives life." It is also said, "Do not have the grime washed off your face and hands by another." Also, "A lantern should not be lit without caution."

99. *Do not become tired of things [duty].*

Mencius[14] said, "If you persevere and do not grow tired of things, you can enter into the ranks of gentleman-scholars."

The above ninety-nine articles are wordy and would be burdensome to others. They are not to be divulged carelessly. They should be regarded as my last testimony to you.

Herein lies the secret oral tradition of the House of Takeda.
Eiroku Gannen [1558], an auspicious day in the fourth month
To the Choro[15]
Nobushige

---

[14] Mencius (371?-289? BC), a philosopher who propagated and advanced Confucius' teachings.

[15] Nobushige's son; Choro is a title used to refer to the eldest son and heir.

*Alexander C. Bennett, a native of New Zealand, began his training in kendo, naginata, and iaido in 1987. He also trains in the classical traditions of Tendo-ryu naginatajutsu and Hoki-ryu iaijutsu. He has translated several important basic martial arts texts from Japanese into English, and has written, in Japanese, for **Budo Gekkan** (Budo Monthly). This text is derived from his master's thesis (University of Canterbury, New Zealand) which was researched at Kyoto University, where he is now a doctoral candidate.*

Neglected Treasure
The Koyo Gunkan

Alexander C. Bennett

Men are your castles
Men are your walls
Compassion is your ally
Malice is your foe

Koyo Gunkan, chapter 40

Modern martial arts students are likely to be familiar with the brilliant military strategist and warlord Takeda Shingen (1521-1573) and the legacy of his clan, the Kai Takeda. The Japanese classical arts of Kogen Itto-ryu kenjutsu, Daito-ryu aikijujutsu, Koshu-ryu gunpo (military strategy), and Takeda-ryu kyubajutsu (mounted archery; also known as *yabusame*) all claim descent from Takeda clan teachings. What many are not aware of is the profound influence the Takeda clan had on the development of the concept of *bushido,* the warrior class ethical system, which in turn can be said to permeate much of modern Japanese culture.

In 1615, Obata Kagenori (1572-1663), son of a Takeda clan military strategist, began to compile a work now known as the *Koyo Gunkan* (甲陽軍鑑), the *Military Chronicles of Kai*. This twenty-volume work, divided into fifty-nine books, included accounts of the Takeda clan's rise and fall; their unique military tactics; the army's constitution; their laws and precepts; and descriptions of their weapons, customs, and lifestyle. Although most of the content is clearly the product of the earlier Sengoku period (1467-1568), the *Koyo Gunkan* came to have enormous influence on the young *bushi* of the peaceful Edo period (1600-1868), who used it as a history, military strategy, and ethics textbook.

Many of the fifty-nine books or chapters are accounts of specific battles fought by the Takeda clan. However, the *Koyo Gunkan* was much more than a simple military chronicle. Its intent appears to have been a desperate plea to Shingen's son, Katsuyori (1546-1582), to show more prudence in dealing with his vassals. This is perhaps expressed most clearly in the "Myogo no Maki."[1] These volumes focused on a detailed analysis of the deportment and responsibilities of both the warriors and their lords and provided explanations of what constituted the ideal warrior or warlord as distinct from the other Japanese classes. This ideal is then contrasted with examples of bad warlords who caused the downfall of their clans.

Just as the content is varied, so too is the style of the individual chapters and volumes. Some sections of the *Koyo Gunkan* were essentially lists entirely written in *kanbun* (classical Chinese writing), such as the house laws (*hatto*) and the family precepts (*kakun*). Other volumes were in epistolary format, such as Naito Shuri's opinions on the laws concerning fighting among the clan warriors. The well-known "Sekisuiji Monogatari" chapter was composed as a series of questions and answers based on conversations between Shingen and his retainers at Sekisui Temple in his home province of Kai. The chapters on battles and military strategy were written in a bland textbook style. Perhaps of greater literary interest, the text also contains many poems composed by Shingen, various retainers, and even his enemies.

The *Koyo Gunkan* subsequently became one of the most important reference works for scholars of bushido throughout the Edo period, when the concept assumed its mature form as a deliberately articulated

---

[1] The *myogo* was a legendary ox with a bladed tail. It was said to lick its tail because it delighted in the taste of its own blood. However, if it overindulged, its tongue was torn to shreds and it bled to death. This behavior is compared, in the "Myogo no Maki" (Myogo Volume), to the deportment of the four types of foolish lords (the foolish lord, the lord who is too clever, the cowardly lord, and the lord who is too strong) who cause the destruction of their family lines and domains. These four chapters (11-14) of detailed descriptions of these incompetent lords are the most often quoted portion of the *Koyo Gunkan*.

SWORD & SPIRIT

ethical system and martial cult. It provided first-hand information on the bushi ethos of the Sengoku period, which was nostalgically admired as the warrior culture's "Golden Age." In fact, the *Koyo Gunkan* was the first text to use the word bushido (武士道) to designate the ruling warrior class' ethical code. In addition to martial prowess, this way of the bushi demanded a sense of honor, loyalty, devotion to duty, courage, and acceptance of the inevitability of death.

Although the term bushido made its first appearance in the *Koyo Gunkan*, the general concept of a special warrior class moral ethos was not new. Other terms such as "*budo*" (武道 "military way"), *samuraido* (侍道 "retainer's way"), and "*dando*" or "*otokodo*" (男道 "man's way") had also been used to describe the appropriate behavior of the bushi in both the *Koyo Gunkan* and earlier texts.

The *Koyo Gunkan* is a massive and often neglected primary source of medieval Japan, and it is a rich source of information on day-to-day life and culture during the Japanese medieval period. A study of the text provides a clear insight into the morality and ethical mindset of the *sengoku* bushi, a factor that made it popular with the later Edo period warrior-class, and thus a major influence in the defining of bushido. It was popular for its vivid depictions of Sengoku period warriors, who were constantly faced with the treachery of shifting alliances and the reality of death in battle. The *Koyo Gunkan* outlined behavior and responsibilities, through direct admonition as well as example, to ensure trust, loyalty, and understanding between the lord and his warriors, hence maximizing the efficiency of the army and guaranteeing the continuation of the domain and clan. The history of the Takeda house suggests that this system's development, at least within the Takeda domain during the golden years of Takeda Shingen, was successful.

A Brief History of the Takeda Clan

The *Koyo Gunkan* centers on the life and times of Takeda Shingen and his son, Takeda Katsuyori. The tale of the Takeda family's rise and fall epitomizes the history of the great Sengoku period clans, and spans nearly eight centuries. In Heian (794-1185) and pre-Heian Japan, extra princes were sometimes removed from the imperial line in a process known as "dynastic shedding." This helped to keep the imperial line free of succession disputes, preserved the lives of the "shed" princes, and reduced the number of imperial family members who required the nation's support. Emperor Seiwa's (850-881) grandson was given the family name of Minamoto, and as Minamoto no Tsunemoto (917-961) founded one of the most illustrious families in Japanese history, the Seiwa Genji.[2] The Takeda family was descended from this line through Shinra Saburo Yoshimitsu (1045-1127); his great-grandson Takeda Nobuyoshi (1128-1186) took as his surname the name of the small village in which he was living in Kai Province (now Yamanashi Prefecture).

The Takeda family was a prominent military house throughout the Kamakura (1185-1333), Muromachi (1333-1568), and Azuchi-Momoyama (1568-1600) periods. Family members played major roles in a number of conflicts, including the Jokyu and Eikyo Disturbances.[3] Takeda Nobutora (1494-1574) finally consolidated the family's position, centered on their stronghold in Kai, and was elevated to the status of *daimyo* (warlord). The house reached its peak under the leadership of Nobutora's son, Takeda Shingen.[4]

Shingen's younger brother, Takeda Nobushige (1525-1561; also known as Takeda Tenkyu), renowned as both scholar and warrior, was favored by their father and had been designated heir to the Takeda domain. Nobutora was not popular with his people or his vassals, so when Shingen took up arms to oust his father, he received widespread support, including that of Nobushige. In 1541, Shingen succeeded in wresting control of the domain from his father. After assuming

[2] "Gen" is merely an alternate reading of the character for Minamoto, while "ji" means family.

[3] The former was an attempt by the retired emperor Go-Toba to overthrow the Kamakura shogunate in Jokyu 3 (1221); the latter, Ashikaga Mochiuji's revolt against the Muromachi shogunate in Eikyo 10 (1438).

[4] He began using the name Shingen after 1559; the name given him at his coming of age ceremony in 1536 was Harunobu.

leadership and securing his position in Kai, he embarked on a campaign of expansion and invaded neighboring Shinano Province (now Nagano Prefecture) in 1542. Shingen easily subdued the many independent landholders (*dogo*) who inhabited this mountainous region, but it was not until 1559 that he was able to conquer the province's farthest reaches. His conquest was then legitimized by the shogun, Ashikaga Yoshiteru (1536-1565), who appointed him *shugo* (provincial military governor) of the region.

Shingen's expansionist policies inevitably brought him into conflict with the man who became his greatest rival, Uesugi Kenshin (1530-1578). Uesugi was the daimyo of Echigo Province (now Niigata Prefecture), and their rivalry is among the most renowned of the Sengoku era. They were involved in perpetual warfare from 1553, with the most famous of their battles being those at Kawanakajima on the Shinano-Echigo border, fought between 1553 and 1564. Shingen's brother, Nobushige, who was referred to as the Takeda *fuku-shogun* (vice warlord), was killed at the age of thirty-seven at the 1561 Battle of Kawanakajima (Sato 117). Although Nobushige was able to stop the enemy advance on Shingen's headquarters before he was overcome, Uesugi outmaneuvered and defeated the Takeda forces (Wilson 100).

In 1554, Shingen formed a trilateral alliance with Imagawa Yoshimoto (1519-1560) of Sumpu (now Shizuoka Prefecture) and Hojo Ujiyasu (1515-1571) of Odawara (now Kanagawa Prefecture) to ensure the security of his southern and eastern borders. However, this alliance began to crumble when Shingen formed a separate alliance with Oda Nobunaga (1534-1582), who had defeated the Imagawa clan at the Battle of Okehazama in 1560. The alliance was dissolved entirely in 1568 when Tokugawa Ieyasu (1543-1616)[5] entered into an agreement with Shingen and Nobunaga to divide up the Imagawa domain, which included

---

[5] Tokugawa Ieyasu (then known as Matsudaira Motoyasu) had been sent, at the age of four, by his father as hostage to the Imagawa clan to cement an alliance. When Ieyasu was eighteen, Oda Nobunaga routed Imagawa Yoshitomo at the battle of Okehazama, thereby freeing Ieyasu. He then returned to his ancestral castle to assume command of his deceased father's former vassals and promptly allied himself with Oda Nobunaga.

Suruga and Totomi (now Shizuoka Prefecture). Shingen then had to fight his former ally, the Hojo of Odawara, to subjugate Suruga. Finally, in 1568, in an attempt to shield himself from future attack, he went so far as to propose a pact with arch-rival Uesugi Kenshin. However, the Hojo foiled his plan by anticipating his move and allying with Uesugi themselves. Eventually, Shingen's aggressive march into Suruga forced Ieyasu to renege on his agreement with Takeda, and he too became a Uesugi ally in 1570.

The next year, while everyone was fighting over the spoils of Totomi, Shingen boldly pressed westward to invade Ieyasu's domain of Mikawa (now Aichi Prefecture). Following this move, Shingen renewed his alliance with the Hojo in 1571, and both once more turned their hostility toward Uesugi. In 1572, he continued westward, allegedly in an attempt to take control of the capital, Kyoto. In the first month of 1573, he soundly defeated the combined forces of Nobunaga and Ieyasu at the Battle of Mikatagahara; then he pressed on to take Noda Castle, situated deep in Tokugawa territory. However, before he could reach Kyoto, he fell gravely ill and died on the thirteenth day of the fourth month of 1573, bringing his campaign and career to an abrupt close.

Although Shingen never completed this campaign, many scholars credit him with causing the Muromachi shogunate's downfall,[6] since it was Shingen's decisive victory at Mikatagahara that encouraged Shogun Ashikaga Yoshiaki (1537-1597) to take up arms against Nobunaga. However, upon Shingen's death, Nobunaga surrounded Kyoto and set fire to the city's periphery. When the capital's upper section was burnt, the shogun surrendered to Nobunaga, and was eventually exiled. The Muromachi shogunate technically continued to exist until Yoshiaki's abdication in 1588, but in reality Nobunaga and his allies controlled the country.

[6] Inoue Toshio and Isogai Masayoshi are two such scholars. The shogunate, or *bakufu* in Japanese, refers to any of the three military governments that ruled Japan from 1192 to 1867, the Kamakura shogunate (1192-1333), the Muromachi shogunate (1338-1573), and the Tokugawa shogunate (1603-1867).

After Shingen's death, Katsuyori inherited the Takeda domain, which now included the provinces of Kai, Shinano, Suruga (now part of Shizuoka Prefecture), Kozuke (now Gumma Prefecture), and Hida (now Gifu Prefecture). Katsuyori was neither a talented administrator nor very popular with the Takeda vassals. Confronted with the mighty enemies Oda Nobunaga and Tokugawa Ieyasu, Katsuyori's situation was precarious. Nevertheless, he continued his father's expansionist policies, fighting against Ieyasu with considerable success in Totomi in 1574. Once he had control of Totomi, he launched an attack on Ieyasu in his home territory, Mikawa Province. However, this move proved ill fated, and the Nobunaga-Ieyasu alliance all but annihilated his force at the Battle of Nagashino in 1575.

Katsuyori was able to regroup after this catastrophe, but his downfall was ensured when his ally, Hojo Ujimasa (1538-1590)of Odawara, switched allegiances and sided with Nobunaga and Ieyasu. Many of Katsuyori's vassals followed suit, whereupon a massive attack was launched on the Takeda domains. Katsuyori fled into the mountains of Kai accompanied by a few loyal retainers, then committed suicide to avoid capture on the third day of the fourth month in 1582. The Takeda territories were distributed among Nobunaga's vassals, and the house of Takeda became extinct.[7]

This brief account of the Takeda family's rise and fall clearly illustrates the chaos and complexity of relationships during the Sengoku era. Alliances were broken as often as they were honored. Treachery occurred with appalling frequency. Codes of conduct and household laws, such as were included in the *Koyo Gunkan*, attempted to counteract these tendencies. Ideally, according to these writings, loyalty was ensured by the lord's correct conduct toward his warriors. Katsuyori's behavior, frequently ignoring the lessons of the *Koyo Gunkan*, caused internal discord within the Takeda clan, leading directly to its fall. Had

---

[7] This outline of the Takeda family history was taken from Itasaka (1983), Arai (1983), and Ota (1995).

he heeded the warnings of his father's advisers, Japanese history might have been much different.

The Koyo Gunkan as Chronicle, and Historical and Philosophical Textbook

The author of *Koyo Gunkan Bengi* (*A Discussion of the Koyo Gunkan*) critically pointed out, "It is not a record, it is not a narrative, and it cannot be viewed as a war diary...."[8] In fact, much of the "history" recounted in the *Koyo Gunkan* does not seem to have ever occurred. The accounts of the Takeda clan's battles during the Sengoku period are particularly unreliable, and there are many historical discrepancies found in the actions and words of Takeda Shingen's main rivals: Uesugi Kenshin, Oda Nobunaga, and Tokugawa Ieyasu. Also, a number of characters in the text appear to be figments of the author's imagination.

Perhaps the most famous of these is Yamamoto Kansuke, a warrior of some renown who was reputed to have only one eye and to be quite physically unattractive. Although he was consequently shunned as an outcast as he traveled throughout the country in search of employment, Takeda Shingen was said to have realized his true worth as a warrior and to have accepted him as a retainer. The *Koyo Gunkan* notes that he was killed at the 1561 Battle of Kawanakajima after making a suicidal attack on the enemy in an act of retribution for a tactical error. Unfortunately, Kansuke only appears in the *Koyo Gunkan* and related texts, and is not explicitly mentioned in any other document of the period, which makes it difficult to confirm that he played such a considerable role in the Takeda army as the *Koyo Gunkan* suggests. For example, one battle in which Yamamoto was said to have played a major part was the Battle of Toishi. The *Koyo Gunkan* says he turned a desperate situation into a Takeda clan victory. However, documents quoted in the *Takeda*

---

[8] Published in 1707. The name of the author is unknown, but it is assumed that he was a hermit who wrote a number of texts concerning the warrior ethos; as quoted in Yoshida (4).

Shingen Den indicate that this battle was actually a crushing defeat for the Takeda.[9]

Today, a number of scholars doubt that Yamamoto ever existed. If he did, it is most likely that he was not one of Shingen's generals but merely a low-ranking *samurai*. Whatever the case, it is interesting that in a military text such as the *Koyo Gunkan* a fictionalized character should be a central figure in so many episodes. One possible reason for creating a heroic character such as Yamamoto Kansuke may have been to emphasize the effectiveness of Takeda military strategy and tactics through an imaginary general who successfully employed these tactics in battle. It would also be convenient to have such a figure take part in various imaginary conversations with Takeda Shingen as a means to depict Shingen's "enlightened" character, such as can be seen with the question-and-answer format between the two in the "Sekisuiji Monogatari" chapter.

A number of battles described in the *Koyo Gunkan* also appear to be fictitious, most notably those recorded in chapters 21 through 23. Three battles attributed to the young Takeda Harunobu (Shingen) — the Battle of Koarama (1540), where he was reputed to have defeated the army of Murakami Yoshikiyo; the Battle of Sezawa (1542), in which he is said to have defeated Ogasawara Choji and Suwa Yorishige; and the Battle of Hirazawa (1542), where he is again alleged to have defeated Murakami Yoshikiyo — are not mentioned in any other surviving documents of the period. Without independent verification outside of the *Koyo Gunkan*, the authenticity of these accounts is in serious doubt (Nitta, Sakaiya, and Ueno, 239).

Despite its historical inaccuracies, the *Koyo Gunkan* was popular enough to prompt analysis and critiques almost as soon as it was completed. Although many famous scholars, such as Ogyu Sorai and Yuasa Jozan, criticized it for these historical discrepancies, there is no doubt that it had a profound influence on the development of the concept of bushido.

[9] Hirose Koichi, quoted in Yoshida (7).

ABOUT THE AUTHOR(S)

No one is really certain who wrote the texts that make up the *Koyo Gunkan*. According to the signature at the end of each chapter, the primary author was Kosaka Danjo Masanobu (1527-1578), son of a farmer, Kasuga Osumi, from Isawa, Kai. At the age of sixteen, Kosaka entered the service of Takeda Shingen, who recognized his talents, and he rapidly rose from retainer to general. He played an important role in systematizing Shingen's political and military theories, and was his most valued counselor. There is evidence to suggest that the two were engaged in a homosexual relationship.[10] Such relationships were far from rare within the bushi class. Further support for the notion of Kosaka as the author can thus be found in the deep love and admiration for Shingen expressed throughout the *Koyo Gunkan*. Kosaka died of illness in 1578, four years before the Takeda clan's downfall.

However, other scholars believe that the man who compiled the *Koyo Gunkan*, Obata Kagenori, was actually the author. The third son of Obata Masamori, Kagenori was a retainer of the Takeda house, and after its demise, he wandered throughout the country as a *ronin* (masterless warrior) studying the art of military science before entering the employ of Tokugawa Ieyasu. After the winter siege of Osaka castle in 1615, he began to work as a spy for the Tokugawa. He was able to enter the castle and make his escape before the beginning of the summer siege later that same year. He then worked openly for the shogunate, teaching the military sciences until his death at age ninety-two.

He organized a system that came to be known as Takeda-ryu gungaku (Takeda-style military science) and in the process apparently gathered considerable information on the Takeda government and military tactics and strategy. He was also clearly responsible for compiling and editing the documents and scripts that make up the *Koyo Gunkan*. In addition, he wrote a number of other renowned military strategy texts such as *Koyo Gunkan Misho* (*Unwritten Koyo Gunkan*), *Shingen*

---

[10] See the letter Takeda Shingen wrote to Kosaka Danjo quoted in Nitta, Sakaiya, and Ueno (230).

Painting of a Takeda clan samurai by Obata Chiura, ca. 1901.

Neglected Treasure

Zenshu (*The Complete Takeda Shingen*), and *Heiho Okugisho* (*The Secret of High Strategy*),[11] some of which were appended to the *Koyo Gunkan*. He evidently signed many of these texts with the names Kosaka Danjo and Yamamoto Kansuke, perhaps in an attempt to legitimize his works and teachings by linking them to the now-legendary warlords of the romantic past. Due to Obata Kagenori's efforts in developing Takeda-ryu military science, the shogunate authorized the style as an official educational curriculum for bushi. In turn, its widespread use led to the popularization of the *Koyo Gunkan* and related texts.

Two opposing factions have arisen in Japanese scholarship, each supporting one of these two men as author of the *Koyo Gunkan*. The Obata Kagenori faction argues that if the author had been Kosaka Danjo, who was actually alive and in the service of Takeda Shingen and his son Katsuyori, there should not be so many fundamental historical errors in the text. Proponents thus claim that the bulk of the *Koyo Gunkan* must have been written by Obata Kagenori, who was only a child when the Takeda house was destroyed, and who would have had access only to second-hand information and accounts.

This assertion, first made as early as 1707 and elaborated upon by Tanaka Gisei in 1891, was refuted by Arima Norisuke in *Koyo Gunkan to Koshu-ryu Heiho* (Ishioka and Arima 224-230). Arima maintained that the main author was indeed Kosaka Danjo, and that the work was completed after Kosaka's death by his nephew, Kasuga Sojiro. He noted that the original text was actually dictated by Kosaka and transcribed by Noh expert Okura Hikojuro. There is evidence to suggest that Obata Kagenori received the collection of Kosaka's writings from his father, who was a high-ranking Takeda retainer, then added his own text, and signed them with Kosaka's name. Obata's later works concentrate mainly on military tactics. While he easily could have been responsible for writing any of the many chapters in the *Koyo Gunkan* that also concern strategy, he was not even born when many of the documented discussions between Shingen and his retainers took place.

---

[11] Attributed to Yamamoto Kansuke; see T. Obata's translation (iv-vii).

Thus, Obata's contributions were most likely the sections on military strategy, whereas the original text appears to have been written by Kosaka Danjo, a retainer who actually existed in the time of Shingen (Nitta, Sakaiya, and Ueno 226-227).

Sakai Kenji's *Koyo Gunkan Taisei* supports this latter argument. I believe that the main author was Kosaka Danjo, who began writing in 1571, followed by his nephew Kasuga Sojiro after Kosaka's death. These writings were then compiled and augmented by Obata Kagenori.

Transmission of the Koyo Gunkan

The original *Koyo Gunkan,* as dictated by Kosaka Danjo, transcribed by Okura Hikojuro, and continued by Kasuga Sojiro, probably did not consist of all the volumes that were eventually organized by Obata Kagenori. In Genna 7 (1621), Obata took the manuscripts his father had passed on to him, arranged them, added some material of his own, and then copied them out as the *Koyo Gunkan*. This original was then duplicated and circulated — to the extent that approximately ten copies made in the seventeenth century have survived to the present, and some twenty editions were circulating during the Edo period (Furukawa 40).

Sorting out the origins and lineages of the various hand-copied manuscripts of the *Koyo Gunkan* is a laborious and complicated task. Sakai Kenji, the scholar responsible for our current knowledge on this subject, has had to rely on some guesswork to reconstruct the relationships between the extant copies (1: 62-96). Naturally, all the books contain the same general content, but they also have their own characteristics and style due to the method in which they were copied, and these characteristics were amplified the further away the copy was from the original.

The most obvious differences between the original manuscript and subsequent copies lie in the use of *kanji*. In the original it is written:

> Although seemingly inappropriate to write this text in
> *kana* [the phonetic syllabary], it is useless to try and revert it
> into kanbun. However, it is permissible to transcribe the

kanbun sections into kana. In such a case, it is desirable that the original kanbun text also be copied and placed with the transcribed kana version.... Kana was primarily used in this text because only one of a hundred men is educated enough to read Chinese text. With this in mind, those young and old who are uneducated will be able to pick this text up on a rainy day and read it (Sakai 1: 30).

While the use of kana alone does allow less literate readers access to the text, it results in ambiguities not found when using kanji, and the copiers of the *Koyo Gunkan* frequently took it upon themselves to interpret the text by applying what they believed to be the appropriate kanji. These attempts to elucidate the meaning were based entirely on the transcriber's guess as to what kanji the kana represented. As a result, we find different kanji applied in different versions of the book. When one is trying to research the underlying, less obvious concepts in the text, or to translate the text, these differences take on greater significance.

Thus, copying out the *Koyo Gunkan* was no simple task. In addition to the problems of deciding which writing system to use, copyists frequently resorted to the phrase *"kono shita kirete miezu"* (following section missing/not legible) to indicate places where there was damage to the original manuscript. The phrase *"kuden ari"* (oral teaching) also appears at various points, referring to places where additional information was supposed to have been passed down directly. More probably, this notation was yet another way the transcriber could deal with text missing from the original.

"Kyujukyu Kakun" and Morality in the Koyo Gunkan

At the *Koyo Gunkan's* thematic heart are the "Kyujukyu Kakun" (Ninety-Nine Precepts), which comprise chapter two of the first volume.[12] They were recorded in 1558 by Takeda Nobushige, Shingen's

---

[12] See pages 17-33 for a complete translation of the "Ninety-Nine Precepts."

younger brother, as a code of conduct for his young son. In some cases, the precepts are very specific guides to behavior, and were used to educate the young bushi in the Takeda domain in much the same way that a Christian child would learn morals from the Bible at Sunday School. Though Nobushige wrote the precepts, it is likely that Shingen himself endorsed them, and all bushi under his command would have been familiar with their content. The prominent themes of the precepts — loyalty to one's lord (Shingen), the importance of recognizing and accomplishing one's duties, modesty, patience, military readiness, human relations, the importance of the master fulfilling his obligations towards his men and domain — are also threaded throughout the sometimes disparate collection of writings that make up the *Koyo Gunkan*, and serve to bind them together into a whole.

The entire chapter, also known as "Takeda Nobushige no Kakun" (The House Precepts of Takeda Nobushige), is written in kanbun and would have represented a substantial reading challenge even for the educated warrior. Confucian thought was a major influence, with each precept reinforced by a relevant quotation from famous Chinese classics such as the *Analects* of Confucius, Wu-tzu, *Shih Chi, San Lüeh, Sun Tzu Ping Fa, Hou Han Shu, Li Chi, Tso Chuan, Shang Shu, Lü Shih Ch'un Ch'iu, Shu Ching, Tao-Te-Ching, Ssu-ma Fa, I Ching, Hsiao Ching*, and Mencius.[13]

The precepts were formulated during an era when the military system was becoming more organized and refined, and ethical principles were formulated to complement the laws of the domain (hatto), also recorded in the *Koyo Gunkan*. The hatto were strict and anyone who broke them was guaranteed punishment, often severe. On the other hand, the house precepts (kakun) were moralistic, and so the interpretation of each depended entirely upon the conscience of the individual. Because moral aspects could not be stressed in legal documents, it was

---

[13] The Wade-Giles Romanization system for Chinese-Mandarin is used in this text because the terms are historical, that is, pre-People's Republic of China. The Pinyin equivalent is provided in the index.

necessary to formulate the kakun. This pattern can also be seen in the domains of the Hojo, Uesugi, and other great military houses (Sato 146).

The formal laws thus complemented the moral precepts, and the combined purpose was to ensure stability in the domain by protecting the interests of government, commerce, and agriculture. They accomplished this task by setting rules and common ethics both for the bushi and their masters, who, entrusted with the task of protecting the domain, needed to be fairly disposed and prudent. This required that they scrutinize their own deportment and dedicate themselves to their duties.

A major characteristic of the precepts was an emphasis on absolute loyalty to one's lord, in this case Shingen, to achieve the paramount goal: preservation of the domain and the family line of its leaders. Ironically, a major criticism of Takeda Shingen by people such as his arch-rival Uesugi Kenshin was his unfilial action of expelling his father Nobutora from Kai. With his "immoral" history of rebelling against his father, how are the "Ninety-Nine Precepts" specifically, and the *Koyo Gunkan* as a whole, able to justify such stress on loyalty to Shingen? Shingen was twenty-one years old when he expelled his father from Kai. If these actions had been carried out purely on a whim, then surely the governing of Kai after such an insurrection would have been unstable. However, as is indicated by comments recorded in the *Koyo Gunkan* by such powerful vassals as Itagaki Nobukata, Nobutora was widely regarded as a tyrant and was an unpopular governor:

> Lord Nobutora conducted himself improperly and indulged in debauchery. He punished both hardened and petty criminals identically. When he was in a bad mood, he punished one and all indiscriminately without discerning who was right or wrong. He rewarded those he liked with stipends, even when they had been treasonous, yet offered no rewards to honest warriors who showed great devotion and loyalty. He handled everything in the opposite manner [to which it should have been]. Everything he did was wrong, so

his son ousted him, even though Nobutora was his father. (Sakai 1: 212)

As this passage suggests, Shingen had a moral duty to purge the domain of such an immoral ruler as Nobutora, and the Takeda vassals supported his efforts. Although such accounts are predictably part of the *Koyo Gunkan*, other texts, such as the *Katsuyama Ki*, also stated that the people of Kai were "overjoyed" with Shingen's expulsion of his tyrannical father (Sato 129). Therefore, although Shingen's rebellion appears to have been immoral, it was considered to be ethical under the circumstances. Besides, he did not go so far as to kill his father. In this respect then, Nobushige did not consider precept 1, "You must not commit treachery against your lord," to apply to Shingen's actions. And even though precept 6 states, "Always be dutiful to your parents," Shingen's vassals did not regard his actions as contradicting this precept. Nevertheless, it is written that Shingen's conscience never allowed him to read the Confucian *Analects* because of his deeds, no matter how righteous his followers proclaimed him to be.

Ironically, in theory, it was Nobushige who posed the biggest threat to Shingen's hegemony, and one would have thought that Shingen would have regarded him with much suspicion. However, Nobushige gave his support to Shingen when he expelled Nobutora, and eventually became one of his most trusted advisers. This gave realization to precept 7, "You should not scheme in even the smallest way against your brothers.... Brothers are your left and right hands." Clearly, Nobushige considered internal stability and unification of both domain and household to be of primary importance, a point Kosaka stressed throughout the *Koyo Gunkan*. Related to this, precept 32, "The retainer must act as a retainer should even if the master does not act as a master should," could be considered very important to Nobushige (despite the obvious contradiction). In times when it was possible for men of low status to overthrow their masters, advocating this precept was a way of assuring the maintenance of Shingen's authority, and is an indication of Nobushige taking the initiative to swear allegiance and loyalty to his brother, Shingen.

As Nobushige was also a warlord in control of vast numbers of warriors, he was aware that his son would inherit his position, and in the future become a central figure in the Takeda army. It is with this in mind that he stressed such precepts as number 22, "Do not neglect loyal retainers…. If the master cannot discern between right and wrong, retainers of merit will lose all interest," as the necessary attitude for a lord. In fact, there are many precepts concerning how a lord or master should treat his men fairly, perhaps a warning that by not doing so, one could meet Nobutora's fate. Also, as stated in precept 31, one is obligated to give retainers a chance, and to educate them regarding right and wrong. Precept 33 warns not to be too strict with one's men, "Too strict a rule will not be observed; too many prohibitions will not be obeyed." Precept 52 stresses the importance of forgiving a retainer for making any mistakes: "A master should forget a retainer's crime if he repents after being admonished." By looking at all the precepts aimed at the lord (or head of the household), one discovers a strong emphasis on the lord as a father figure to his retainers. The lord was to avoid becoming too aloof and to retain a paternal quality, as well as a sense of equality, in order to gain and maintain the respect of his retainers and subjects. This ideal of benevolence on behalf of the lord toward his men is clearly demonstrated in precept 57, "When there were consignments of food and wine, a great commander of old would pour the wine into the river and drink [water] with his men."

As far as military affairs are concerned, the lord must be seen to be confident and charismatic enough to be able to encourage his men to be valorous and accomplish their duties. It is often stated that Nobushige's "Ninety-Nine Precepts" are focused mainly on ethical issues, but there are also numerous references to strategy and correct deportment of soldiers and lords alike in the face of battle. Each had their own responsibilities, and it was their "moral duty" to perform them to the best of their ability to enable the domain's continuation and prosperity. "When one's allies are on the verge of defeat, one should be roused to fight all the more. In the *Ku-Liang Chuan* it says, 'If your strategy is thoughtfully prepared, you need not fight. However, if you must fight and do it well, you will not perish'" (precept 73).

The final precept states, "Do not become tired of things [duty]." This expresses again the need for absolute devotion and loyalty to the lord (or vice versa), and relentless service without negligence, and can be called the main theme of the "Ninety-Nine Precepts, and indeed the central theme of the *Koyo Gunkan.*

In summary, the ideal warlord and warrior as described in the *Koyo Gunkan* was to be martially capable and able to show discretion. He should strive to be "manly" and avoid bad company, such as the polluting influences of financially minded merchants, by being aware of his obligations and the duties of his profession. He should be loyal to the point of death to his lord, and reliable both in battle and during times of peace. The warlord also had obligations as role model and pseudo-father to his subordinates. Both would work to maintain the prosperity and continuation of the domain and family by maintaining close emotional bonds. The warrior should be modest and avoid showing off. He was also expected to be an individual who was honest, sincere, and frank with himself and others, including his lord. Both should also be well-rounded individuals who would be versed in all manner of etiquette, but would avoid extremes. Their ultimate duty was to ensure the domain's survival.

Conclusion

The early Edo period bushi, especially those who had first-hand experience in the battles of the Sengoku period, tried to retain the values derived from their professional duties as warriors in battle. The most important of these were the accomplishment of valorous deeds (*tegara*) and the consequent honor that accrued to one's name. A reputation based on the gallant deeds on the battlefield was the foundation for group and individual identity of the bushi prior to the Edo period. The swords they carried, their martial skills, and battlefield experience set them apart from the other classes and professions.[14] Thus, the most

---

[14] This became even more so after the "sword hunt" ordered by Toyotomi Hideyoshi (1537-1598) in 1588 prohibited non-samurai from owning weapons. Hideyoshi

highly cherished bushi ethical qualities were directly related to their function as professional warriors.

Japan's medieval period ended with Tokugawa Ieyasu's victory at Sekigahara in 1600, which brought the period of incessant civil war of the sixteenth century to a close. Within the next fifty years, the shogunate's "Great Peace in the Realm" policies united the nation and brought peace to the war-ravaged land. This resulted in a diminished need for the military services of the ruling bushi class, and warriors lost the opportunity to demonstrate their martial prowess, and hence the chance to enhance their reputation and social standing. The newly developing Tokugawa society did not require military efficiency as much as it needed bureaucratic skills, and the bushi were gradually transformed into bureaucratic administrators.

In response to these drastic changes in their role, the bushi were forced to re-evaluate the very basis of their existence. The battlefield was no longer the measure by which they could prove their worth. However, maintaining their position at the top of the Tokugawa social structure required a distinctive value system to set them apart from the other classes. The ensuing "bushi identity crisis" was also fueled by pressures from the merchants, who had begun to flourish once a lasting peace was established. The warriors were looking for an identity that would serve them in this new society as they performed their new functions, yet would also preserve their traditional warrior values to the greatest extent possible.

Thus, the early Tokugawa bushi strove to maintain a direct link with their battlefield heritage while acknowledging the need to adapt and change to a new era of peace. Drawing on texts such as the *Koyo Gunkan*, they developed a "new version" of bushido by extracting the principle values expressed by these Sengoku-era writings, then applying them to existing social conditions (Fukushima 54). The *Koyo Gunkan*

---

completed the work begun by Oda Nobunaga for national reunification. His famous sword hunt was aimed at reducing the likelihood of armed rebellion, and separating the peasants from the warrior class.

itself thus influenced a whole new crop of texts on the subject and stimulated academic discussion on the merit of the ideals it espoused. Such famous warriors as Tokugawa Ieyasu, who was known to be a great admirer of Shingen, endorsed many of the *Koyo Gunkan*'s teachings (Nitta, Sakaiya, and Ueno 189). Also, in later famous Edo period texts concerning bushido, such as *Budo Shoshinshu* (*The Code of the Samurai*) by Daidoji Yuzan (1639-1730), and *Hagakure* (*Hidden by the Leaves*) by Yamamoto Tsunetomo (1659-1719), there were many references to *Koyo Gunkan* values.

This vision of the ideal warrior was deliberately refashioned during the Edo period to place a greater emphasis on loyalty, self-sacrifice, and fortitude. It was this version of bushido that was distorted by the militant right-wing nationalists to drive Japanese military aggression in this century. The *Koyo Gunkan* and the "Ninety-Nine Precepts" are often overlooked in modern studies of Japanese history and culture because of the number of historical errors contained within the text, yet they offer a clear insight into the workings and motives of a very important class in medieval Japan. This class and period was also the source of the classical martial traditions that continue to be practiced today. Thus, these annals of the Takeda clan offer clues to both scholar and martial artist, and they represent an invaluable primary source.

References

Arai M. 1983. *Takeda Shigen*. Tokyo: Obunsha.

Blomberg, C. 1994. *The Heart of the Warrior: Origins and Religious Background of the Samurai System in Feudal Japan*. Sandgate, England: Japan Library.

Fukushima, S. 1984. "Bushido in Tokugawa Japan: A Reassessment of the Warrior Ethos." Ph.D. dissertation, University of California, Berkeley.

Furukawa T. 1989. Budo no Koten o Megutte (Study on Classic Books of Budo). *The First International Seminar of Budo Culture: Report*, 40-45. Tokyo: Nippon Budokan Foundation.

Haramoto T. 1990. *Koyo Gunkan*. Tokyo: Kyoikusha.

Ikegami, E. 1995. *The Taming of the Samurai: Honorific Individualism and the Making of Modern Japan*. Cambridge, MA: Harvard University Press.

Ishioka H. and Arima S., ed. 1967. *Koyo Gunkan to Koshu-ryu Heiho*. Nippon Heiho Zenshu, vol. 1. Tokyo: Shinjinbutsu Oraisha.

Isogai M. 1963. *Takeda Shingen no Subete*. Tokyo: Jinbutsu Oraisha.

———. 1965. *Koyo Gunkan*. Sengoku Shiryo Sosho, vols. 3-5. Tokyo: Jinbutsu Oraisha.

Itasaka G., chief ed. 1983. *Kodansha Encyclopedia of Japan*. Tokyo: Kodansha.

Masuda K., ed. 1974. *Kenkyusha's New Japanese-English Dictionary*. 4th ed. Tokyo: Kenkyusha.

Mathews, R.H. 1931. *Mathew's Chinese-English Dictionary*. Cambridge, MA: Harvard University Press.

Nitta J., Sakaiya T., and Ueno H. 1988. *'Furinkazan' no Teiogaku: Takeda Shingen*. Tokyo: Purejidentosha.

Ono S., Satake A., and Maeda K., ed. 1990. *Iwanami Kogo Jiten*. Tokyo: Iwanami Shoten.

Ota A., ed. 1995. *Takeda Shingen: Furinkazan no Daisenryaku*. Tokyo: Gakken.

Sagara T. 1969. *Koyo Gunkan — Gorin (no) Sho — Hagakure Shu.* Nippon no Shiso, vol. 9. Tokyo: Chikuma Shobo.

Sakai K. 1995. *Koyo Gunkan Taisei.* 4 vols. Tokyo: Namiko Shoin.

Sato K. 1977. *Sengoku Busho no Kakun.* Tokyo: Shinjinbutsu Oraisha.

Sawyer, R. 1993. *The Seven Military Classics of Ancient China.* Boulder, CO: Westview Press.

Shinmura I., ed. 1994. *Kojien.* 4th ed. Tokyo: Iwanami Shoten.

Tanaka G. 1891. Koyo Gunkan Ko. *Shigakkai Zasshi* 14.

Wilson, W.S. 1982. *Ideals of the Samurai: Writings of the Japanese Warriors.* Burbank, CA: Ohara Publications.

Yamamoto K. 1994. *Heiho Okugisho: The Secret of High Strategy* Translated by T. Obata. Hollywood, California: W.M. Hawley Publications.

Yoshida Y. 1987. *Koyo Gunkan.* Tokyo: Tokuma Shoten.

Meik and Diane Skoss first met in Tokyo in late 1988, when Diane was doing research for an article on naginata. They began to train together in jukendo in 1990, and they were married in 1992. They now train together in jukendo/tankendo, Shinto Muso-ryu jojutsu, and Toda-ha Buko-ryu naginatajutsu. During their time in Japan they attended or participated in countless demonstrations of the classical traditions. These experiences, supplemented by Meik's extensive library of Japanese research material, provide the basis for this "Field Guide."

FIELD GUIDE TO THE CLASSICAL JAPANESE MARTIAL ARTS

Meik & Diane Skoss

This is a continuation of the "Field Guide" chapter in *Koryu Bujutsu: Classical Warrior Traditions of Japan*. We've expanded the entries a bit, but the goal is still to provide a quick reference rather than an in-depth analysis. This "Field Guide" is intended as a tool to enhance your understanding of the classical traditions, and as a companion to demonstrations of these arts, whether live or on video. The *ryu* are listed here in reverse alphabetical order (just as a change of pace). Selections have been made based on the overall content of this book and the quality of the photographs available.

If you are interested in more of the "whys" and "wherefores" of the "Field Guide," please refer to the first installment in *Koryu Bujutsu* (also posted on the web at http://www.koryubooks.com/library/dskoss5.html).

References

Executive Committee for the 600th Birthday Anniversary Celebration of the Founder of the Ryu, Izasa Choisai Ienao. 1987. *Tenshin Shoden Katori Shinto-ryu Kinen-shi: Ryuso Izasa Choisai Ienao-Ko Seitan Roppyakunen wo Kinen Shite* (Memorial Program of the 600th Birthday Anniversary Celebration of the Founder of the Ryu, Izasa Choisai Ienao). Sawara, Chiba: Tenshin Shoden Katori Shinto-ryu.

Kawauchi T. 1954. *Kaicho Zoho: Nihon Budo Ryuso-den* (Traditions and Founders of the Japanese Martial Arts). Tokyo: Nihon Kobudo Shinkokai Jimukyoku.

Miyazaki M., ed. 1994. *Nihon Densho Bugei Ryuha: Dokuhon* (Japanese Traditional Martial Arts Schools: A Handbook). Tokyo: Shinjinbutsu Oraisha.

Nihon Kobudo Kyokai. 1991. *Dai Juyonkai Zen Nihon Kobudo Embu Taikai* (Fourteenth Annual All-Japan Classical Martial Arts Demonstration). Tokyo: Nippon Budokan.

Nihon Kobudo Kyokai. 1998. *Dai Nijuichikai Zen Nihon Kobudo Embu Taikai* (Twenty-first Annual All-Japan Classical Martial Arts Demonstration). Tokyo: Nippon Budokan.

Nitto M., ed. 1978. *Nihon Kobudo no Zenyo* (The Complete Story of the Japanese Classical Martial Arts). Tokyo: Nippon Budokan.

Skoss, D., ed. 1997. *Koryu Bujutsu: Classical Warrior Traditions of Japan*. Berkeley Heights, NJ: Koryu Books.

Watatani K. and Yamada T. 1978. *Bugei Ryuha Daijiten* (Dictionary of Japanese Martial Art Traditions). Tokyo: Tokyo Kopii Shuppanbu.

YOSHIN-RYU
楊心流

Systems/weapons: naginatajutsu; sojutsu (nagayari; tanso);
bojutsu (hanbo); kusarigamajutsu
Date founded: early Tokugawa period (ca. 1660)
Founder: Akiyama Shirobei Yoshitoki
Present representative: Koyama Takako, 13th headmaster
Prefecture: Hiroshima

Field notes: Yoshin-ryu hyoho was originally a comprehensive system
that included *kenjutsu, bojutsu, naginatajutsu, kusarigamajutsu, sojutsu*
(using both long and short spears), and *yawara* (or *jujutsu*), for which
the ryu was most widely known. Additionally, Yoshin-ryu is said to
have had quite an extensive curriculum of methods for treating injuries
and illnesses, perhaps a reflection of the fact that the founder, Akiyama
Shirobei, was a physician who had learned methods of both fighting
and healing while studying in China. As it is practiced today in Hiroshima, the Yoshin-ryu is a weapons school that concentrates on
naginata, hanbo, kusarigama, and *yari.* Naginata techniques are performed against *tachi* and naginata. Other weapons operate against the
tachi. The bojutsu uses a short staff called a hanbo, representing a
naginata that has been broken in combat.

Yoshin-ryu naginatajutsu was used to train ladies-in-waiting and
other maidservants of the feudal lords of the Yanagawa domain (in
present-day Fukuoka Prefecture); exponents typically wear *furisode*
(long-sleeved) kimono, along with white *hachimaki* (headbands) and
tabi (split-toed socks). They bind up their sleeves with a *tasuki* (re-
straining cord or strap). Many Yoshin-ryu techniques end with the exponent standing with their weight on their forward leg and the rear
heel raised well off the ground in what appears to be an awkward position. Although a kimono can be quite restrictive or cramped,
Yoshin-ryu exponents learn to move easily within its confines by

Finish of a naginata tachi awase technique, demonstrated at the 20th Kobudo Demonstration, Nippon Budokan, February 1997.

Sword & Spirit

making use of adroit foot movements, forward and backward and to both sides, as well as twisting actions of the body, achieving maximum effect with minimum movement. Particular attention is given to using the entire length of the naginata, with the haft as a lever, to apply centrifugal force.

Yoshin-ryu techniques will frequently use the opponent's power to turn around, deflect, or sweep away their weapon, then counterattack with the blade, point, or butt-end. Preferred targets are the carotid artery and solar plexus for thrusting attacks; the knee and elbow joints for cutting; and the face, shins, torso, and hands for striking.

An oral teaching of the founder says, "Be graceful like the willow. If the enemy cuts your flesh, finish him by cutting to his bones."

TODA-HA BUKO-RYU
戸田派武甲流

Systems/weapons: naginatajutsu (su naginata, kagitsuki naginata,
nagamaki); kenjutsu; sojutsu; bojutsu; kusarigamajutsu
Date founded: late Muromachi period (ca. 1560)
Founder: Toda Seigen
Present representative: Nitta Suzuo (actual name is Suzuyo; all female
headmasters add a male suffix to their name), 19th headmaster
Prefecture: Tokyo

Field notes: Toda Seigen, and his younger brother, Kagemasa, were
members of a famous family of Chujo-ryu swordsmen. Seigen was especially noted for his ability with the short sword. Because of their out-
standing abilities, their art came to be called the Toda-ryu. The name
was changed to its present form, Toda-ha Buko-ryu, under its thirteenth headmaster, Suneya Ryosuke Takeyuki, although the exact reason is unknown. Suneya was also a well-known teacher of Kogen
Itto-ryu kenjutsu, serving as the official instructor to the Mizuno family in southern Kii (present-day Wakayama Prefecture); he introduced
some of the Buko-ryu naginata *tachi awase* techniques into one line of
that school. Kiraku-ryu, now located in Gumma Prefecture, and especially noted for its *jujutsu, bojutsu, kusarigamajutsu,* and *chigirikijutsu,*
also split off from the original Toda-ryu during the mid-Edo period.

Buko-ryu techniques are predominately designed for battlefield combat, with the movements performed as though the exponents were
wearing armor. Originally a comprehensive system centered on the
sword, the *naginata* is now the major weapon. It is used against the
naginata, *tachi, yari,* and, in an unusual combination, *kusarigama.*
Nagamaki techniques are noted for their reliance on controlling the
maai and abrupt changes of position.

Buko-ryu is one of only two extant ryu using the *kagitsuki* naginata,
a glaive mounted with a cross-bar, which is used to deflect, hook, trap,

SWORD & SPIRIT

Final movement of a kagitsuki naginata tachi awase technique. Soke Nitta Suzuyo, ukedachi, with Meik Skoss, shidachi. Kumano Hayatama Shrine, Shingu City, Memorial Demonstration for Suneya Ryosuke Takeyuki, August 1995.

and cover the opponent's sword or spear. This weapon is the highest level of training at present. The Buko-ryu bojutsu is based upon the assumption that the naginata has been broken in combat and the *shidachi* (performer of the technique) uses what remains of the haft to defeat his opponent. Buko-ryu kusarigama training is divided into two sections. Against the naginata, the techniques are meant to serve as a means of

Final movement of a naginata yari awase technique. Diane Skoss, shidachi, with Meik Skoss, ukedachi. 20th Kobudo Demonstration, Nippon Budokan, February 1997.

training the *ukedachi* (person who is receiving the technique, acting as the opponent) to observe and control the distancing and timing. Against the tachi, the chain-and-sickle operates in a more combative manner, with special emphasis on *irimi* (entering movements) and the use of the *kusari* (chain) and *fundo* (weight) to disrupt the opponent's maai and defeat him.

SWORD & SPIRIT

Tenshin Shoden Katori Shinto-ryu

天真正伝香取神道流

Systems/weapons: kenjutsu (odachi, kodachi, ryoto); iaijutsu (odachi); bojutsu (rokushaku bo); naginatajutsu (onaginata); sojutsu (su yari); jujutsu; shurikenjutsu; ninjutsu; chikujojutsu; gunbaiho; in-yo kigaku
Date founded: early Muromachi period (ca. 1447)
Founder: Iizasa Choisai Ienao
Present representative: Iizasa Yoshisada, 20th headmaster
Prefecture: Chiba

Field notes: Katori Shinto-ryu is generally believed to be the oldest extant Japanese martial tradition and is certainly one of those that has best preserved its comprehensive curriculum. The founder, Iizasa Choisai, served the Chiba family for many years and took part in many battles. In the end, he became disenchanted with the purposes for which martial arts were then being used. He went to Katori Shrine, in Chiba Prefecture, to undertake a regimen of martial and religious training. After one thousand days, he received an insight into the essential nature of the martial arts, which was the basis for what has come to be known as the Tenshin Shoden Katori Shinto-ryu.

Unlike many later creations, which tended to specialize in one or another weapon or on a narrow aspect of the martial arts, the Katori Shinto-ryu curriculum contains a very wide, if not complete, range of martial technique and strategy. The emphasis is on the warrior's central weapon, the sword. With only a few exceptions, the opponent is armed with an *odachi* or long sword, as they believe it to be the fastest, strongest, and most versatile weapon in the warrior's arsenal. Other weapons are studied on the theory that a warrior might face them or be temporarily separated from his sword and have to resort to a "secondary" weapon.

There are nineteen *kata* for the sword, divided into three sets for the odachi (long sword), four for *ryoto* (long and short swords used together), and three for the *kodachi* (short sword). *Iaijutsu* is studied thoroughly, with sixteen techniques, divided into three sets. The next part of the curriculum is *bojutsu*, with six *omote* and six *ura* techniques. The Katori Shinto-ryu *naginata* is notable for its size and weight — it is not a weapon that would have only been used by women as is commonly believed — and there are seven techniques in this section. *Sojutsu* is an advanced level of training in Shinto-ryu; there are six techniques. Although seldom seen, the *jujutsu* portion of the curriculum is quite extensive, with thirty-six techniques that cover a range of techniques from those used for the battlefield to those for self-defense on the street.

Katori Shinto-ryu kata are noted for very long and complex movement sequences that contain a great many applications and variations not evident to an outside observer. Most are performed against an opponent armed with an odachi. Although most of the techniques with the major battlefield weapons (sword, glaive, and spear) can — or are meant to — be performed in armor, others are intended for use while wearing everyday clothing. Shinto-ryu techniques can be adapted to indoors or out, used on smooth and uneven terrain, in the dark, and facing either single or multiple opponents.

In addition to the better known fighting techniques, both unarmed and armed, the Katori Shinto-ryu maintains as an important part of its curriculum the study of strategy and tactics (*gunbaiho*), fortification (*chikujojutsu*), espionage (*ninjutsu*), and esoteric religion and divination (*mikkyo* and *in-yo kigaku*). However, these are studied only at advanced levels, and are seldom seen even by those in the ryu who are less experienced, not to mention people outside the school.

In spite of the strength of the Katori Shinto-ryu techniques and its effectiveness on the battlefield, the current teacher, Otake Risuke, feels that perhaps its most important teaching is very different from what is normally considered typical of the martial arts, *"Heiho wa heiho nari"* (the methods of war are the methods of peace).

Kyoso Shigetoshi, son of Otake Risuke Shihan, demonstrating an iaijutsu technique at Katori Shrine, Chiba, April 1997.

Field Guide to the Classical Japanese Martial Arts   69

TATSUMI-RYU
立身流

Systems/weapons: kenjutsu (odachi, kodachi, nito, fukuro shinai); iai
(odachi); yawara; sojutsu; bojutsu (rokushaku bo, hanbo);
shurikenjutsu; hojojutsu; shudan sentoho; monomi
Date founded: late Muromachi period (ca. 1550)
Founder: Tatsumi Sankyo
Present representative: Kato Takashi, 21st headmaster[1]
Prefecture: Chiba

Field notes: Tatsumi-ryu hyoho is a comprehensive martial art. It encompasses all of the classical warrior's major fighting arts, from swordsmanship (*kenjutsu* and *iai*) and grappling, in and out of armor and with and without weapons (*yawara*), to the use of the spear, long and short staff, and glaive (*sojutsu*, *bo* and *hanbojutsu*, and *naginatajutsu*). It also includes such esoteric subjects as strategy and tactics (*shudan sentoho*), reconnaissance (*monomi*), as well as a host of other teachings about different aspects of warrior culture and philosophy.

The sword is central to Tatsumi-ryu practice and even the use of other weapons, such as the *yari*, *naginata*, *bo*, and *hanbo*, is undertaken with the aim of enabling the swordsman to defeat them. Tatsumi-ryu iai (the ryu does not call its sword-drawing *iaijutsu*) is very simple but elegant, and is based on two techniques that can be performed either standing or seated and in all four directions. *Muko* is an example of *go no sen*, or reactive initiative (the exponent responds to and counters an the opponent's attack). *Marui* can be done in either *sen no sen* or *sensen no sen* fashion (simultaneous or preemptive/proactive initiative), with the swordsman responding either at the same instant as the opponent's

---

[1] See "Kato Takashi: Reflections of the Tatsumi-ryu Headmaster" in *Koryu Bujutsu: Classical Warrior Traditions of Japan*, page 143-153.

Kato Hiroshi (left), demonstrating habiki kenjutsu with his father, Soke Kato Takashi, at Boso no Mura, Chiba, 1991.

attack or forestalling him by attacking first. In Tatsumi-ryu training, *tachiai waza* (standing techniques) are the most important; *igumi waza* (seated techniques) are considered secondary.

The *omote* (basic) level techniques can all be performed at three levels: *jo, ha,* and *kyu.* Jo is used to develop proper habits of movement, and is slow and precise; ha is more fluid and includes more practical applications; and kyu is quite rapid and most resembles techniques as they would be used in actual combat. *Kage* (advanced) techniques are also divided into three levels: *shoden, honden,* and *betsuden.* The kage techniques do not have any blocking movements and are all performed as sen no sen or sensen no sen.

Training is normally done with *bokuto,* but a *fukuro shinai* (training sword made of split bamboo and covered with leather) is sometimes used in kenjutsu to enable the trainee to strike hard without fear of injuring the other person. The *kokyu* (breath control) training in these techniques is particularly strong. *Kodachi* techniques, especially against the yari, place great emphasis on breathing, distancing, trajectory, and the use of *irimi* (entering movements), allowing the exponent to deflect the longer weapon and enter to strike the opponent at will. A further noteworthy characteristic of Tatsumi-ryu kenjutsu technique is the manner in which exponents move rapidly, as though running on an icy surface, allowing them to develop a high level of sensitivity to the opponent's timing, a good sense of balance, and an extraordinary ability to change directions in an instant.

Tatsumi-ryu's yawara component includes unarmed techniques as well as methods of using the long and short swords to control or defeat the opponent. There are forty-five techniques and teachings listed in the *mokuroku,* but many of these have six or more variations, both for armored combat on the battlefield and for while the exponent is wearing regular clothing. Other items in the curriculum are not physical techniques, *per se;* these consist of detailed information warriors needed to know about close combat. Techniques are performed in a very upright, dignified manner, with exquisite timing and application.

TAKENOUCHI-RYU
竹内流

Systems/weapons: jujutsu (torite, koshi no mawari, kogusoku); hade; bojutsu (rokushaku bo, jo); kenjutsu (odachi, kodachi, tanto, aikuchi/kaiken); iaijutsu (odachi, kodachi, tanto, aikuchi/kaiken); hojojutsu (hobaku); naginatajutsu; tessenjutsu; sakkatsuho
Date founded: late Muromachi period (1532)
Founder: Takenouchi Chunagon Daijo Hisamori
Present representatives: Takenouchi Toichiro Hisamune, 14th headmaster; Takenouchi Tojuro Hisatake, 13th sodenke
Prefecture: Okayama

Field notes: Although Takenouchi-ryu is known as one of the oldest martial schools of grappling and close combat in and out of armor, it is in fact a comprehensive system, with a wide range of weapons arts.

According to its traditions, the founder, Takenouchi Hisamori (who has been described in one source as "a long sword walking along with a short man beside it"), was engaged in martial training and religious austerities at the Atago Shrine near his castle. He had been practicing with a *bokuto* some two-*shaku*, four-*sun* in length (about two feet four inches), but was not making much progress. One night, as he slept, a *yamabushi* (mountain ascetic) appeared to him in a dream. He took this figure to be a manifestation of the Atago Shrine deity since it was some seven shaku tall and very fierce looking. Hisamori attacked, but he was helpless. The yamabushi took his bokuto, told him longer weapons were not very useful in combat, and broke it into two pieces, each one-shaku, two-sun in length. He then explained to him how, wearing a short weapon like this, it was possible to engage an enemy in close combat and defeat him. This was the creation of what has come to be known as *koshi no mawari* (lit. "around the hips," referring to the small weapons usually carried in the belt). The deity also showed Hisamori how to use a vine wrapped around the tree to subdue an

Takenouchi Tojuro Hisatake, left, performing a bojutsu technique on Kanzaki Masaru at a demonstration at Meiji Shrine, Tokyo, November 1995.

SWORD & SPIRIT

enemy, giving him the principles of the arrest-and-seizure techniques now known as *hobaku* or *hojojutsu*. Then, according to the *densho* (transmission scrolls), the deity disappeared in a gust of wind and a flash of light. This was recorded as occurring on 26 June 1532 and, even now, a special ceremony is held on that day to commemorate the ryu's founding.

Takenouchi-ryu's second and third headmasters were the second son of Hisamori, Hitachinosuke Hisakatsu, and Kaganosuke Hisayoshi (Hisakatsu's eldest son), both of whom assisted their fathers from a very young age, later adding their own techniques to complete the curriculum. Under the eighth headmaster, in an effort to ensure that the family bloodline and traditions would be preserved, the Takenouchi family split into two lines. The eldest son and heir took the name Tojuro and became the *sodenke* (holder of the complete transmission of the Takenouchi-ryu); a younger son kept the older name of Toichiro, and the formal position of *soke* (headmaster).

There are more than five hundred techniques in the Takenouchi-ryu curriculum, surely one of the largest bodies of martial technique created in Japan. Beginning with unarmed grappling techniques (*torite* and koshi no mawari), unarmed sparring and striking (*hade*), and methods of tying up and subduing an enemy (hojojutsu), trainees go on to learn to use the long and short swords and dagger (in Takenouchi-ryu, the techniques using these three weapons together are called *saite*), sword-drawing (*battoiai*), fighting with a long or short staff (*bo* and *jo*), the glaive (*naginata*), and methods of using the body's vital points for assaulting or restoring another person (*sakkatsuho*).

One of the Takenouchi-ryu's most striking features is how the techniques go from one to another system or art, using whatever weapon or technique is appropriate to the situation. An empty-handed grappling technique segues into the use of a dagger, then changes to more grappling, and finishes with the use of the tying cord and the opponent's submission. In many of the techniques, the initiative changes back and forth between the opponents.

SHOJITSU KENRI KATAICHI-RYU
初実剣理方一流

Systems/weapons: battokenjutsu [yoroi kumitachi, katchu iaijutsu, suhada kenjutsu] (odachi); jojutsu
Date founded: early Tokugawa period (ca. 1680)
Founder: Imaeda Sachu Ryodai
Present representative: Uetsuki Motomu, 17th headmaster
Prefecture: Okayama

Field notes: Imaeda Ryodai began to learn the family art of Imaeda-ryu kenjutsu and battojutsu at the age of ten, after several years of training and education at a Zen temple, the Daigakuin. He was a talented student and made great progress. He then traveled to different parts of Japan to improve his understanding and broaden his skills. When he was in his late teens, he went to Edo to train with his uncle, a retainer of the lord of Omi (present-day Shiga Prefecture). Imaeda became a retainer of the Nagai family, the lords of Settsu (present-day Hyogo Prefecture) for a time, but resigned his position and set out once again on *musha shugyo* (itinerant warrior's training). Eventually, he combined the Imaeda family art with the teachings of Kito-ryu, Kashiwabara-ryu, and a number of other schools to create Shojitsu Kenri Kataichi-ryu.

The Shojitsu Kenri Kataichi-ryu is noted for its techniques of drawing the sword in armor (*katchu iaijutsu* — depicted on the cover), especially its *nukiage* draw, where the blade is reversed so that the cutting edge faces downward and makes an upwards cut as it is drawn. This lets an exponent directly attack the weak points in an enemy's armor or, if performed against an assailant in regular clothing, attack the arteries of the leg or arms or other vital points. The *yoroi kumitachi* techniques include methods of throwing or tripping an opponent as well as in-fighting, when neither man can easily use his longer weapons. They are very effective as *suhada kenpo* (unarmored swordsmanship) as well, and are also practiced in that manner. Another very characteristic

Kanzaki Masaru pausing to let the "blood drain off" after he has performed a todome movement on his fallen opponent. 20th Kobudo Demonstration, Nippon Budokan, February 1997.

movement of the school is a thrust called *todome* (stopping), delivered to the fallen opponent's groin or abdomen to ensure that he is completely finished. Unlike many iai schools, rather than performing the action known as *chiburi* (a movement where the blade is swung sharply around the head to "shake off the blood"), the sword is cleaned by wiping the blade between thumb and forefinger.

Shojitsu Kenri Kataichi-ryu jojutsu is done *suhada* (unarmored) and is intended as a means of self-defense when one is not armed with a sword. There are ten techniques: five against a sword, five against another stick.

SHINTO MUSO-RYU
神道夢想流

Systems/weapons: jojutsu; kenjutsu (odachi, kodachi, nito)
Date founded: early Tokugawa period (ca. 1640)
Founder: Muso Gonnosuke Katsuyoshi
Present representative: No headmaster or single representative is
recognized; a number of teachers who hold the highest level of license
(menkyo kaiden) are teaching in separate groups that interact loosely
Prefecture: all over Japan; the main centers are in Fukuoka, Tokyo, the
Osaka/Kyoto area, Kanagawa, and Aichi

Field notes: Shinto (or Shindo, either pronunciation is correct)
Muso-ryu is said to be the oldest method for using the stick in combat.
It was founded by Muso Gonnosuke Katsuyoshi, a well-known exponent of Shinto-ryu kenjutsu and bojutsu. He is supposed to have
fought Miyamoto Musashi with a staff in a training match and been
defeated by Musashi's *jujidome* (x-block). Dissatisfied with this out-
come, Muso retired to Mt. Homan in what is now Fukuoka Prefecture,
where he engaged in a series of religious austerities, all the while con-
templating the reasons for his defeat. Finally, he received "divine" inspiration about a new method of using a staff-like weapon, making it
shorter and thinner for more rapid manipulation. He devised a number
of techniques for this new weapon, which he called a stick (*jo* or *tsue*),
as opposed to a staff (*bo*). Documents of the *ryu* are quite rare. One record at Tsukuba Shrine, in Ibaragi Prefecture, states that Gonnosuke
was able to defeat Musashi in a rematch, but this story is not recorded
elsewhere, so it is somewhat suspect.

Muso-ryu jojutsu is divided into a number of discrete sets, each with
a different character. Training is systematic and develops the exponent's technical skills and psychological abilities, from body movement
and weapons handling to use of timing and distancing, and intense
mental or spiritual training, all to enable him to successfully use the

SWORD & SPIRIT

Zanshin. Quintin Chambers acting as uchidachi (left), with Phil Relnick, shidachi, at the International Jodo Federation gathering in Hawaii, 1994.

weapon in mortal combat. Trainees now begin their study of jo by learning a set of twelve basic techniques, *kihon waza*, which contain all of the style's essential movements. They then proceed through different sets of techniques of stick versus sword(s): *omote, chudan, ran-ai, kage, sammidare, gohon no midare*, and ending in *okuden*. A final set, the *gokui hiden* (also called *go muso no jo*) consists of techniques that are taught only to people who have received a *menkyo kaiden*, the style's highest level license.

Most of the sets date from the early- through middle-Tokugawa period (early- to middle-16th through middle-17th centuries), shortly after the ryu was created. The two ran-ai techniques appear to date from the middle- or late-Tokugawa period and the five gohon no midare techniques were introduced sometime in the middle of the twentieth

Kage no ukan technique: the man with the stick has just
forestalled Hagiwara Taro's sword thrust.
Meiji Shrine, November 1997.

century. All of the sets contain twelve techniques, plus the occasional variation, except for sammidare, which has five (or six, depending on how one counts) and gohon no midare, with five.

The last level of technique that is generally learned by trainees, okuden, has two sections. Twelve techniques involve the use of the stick against the sword and these are what are commonly referred to as *oku* or okuden. The second oku section involves the use of the long and short swords against another sword. In the *densho* (transmission scrolls), they are listed only as "twelve [techniques for] long sword" and "four [techniques for] short sword," but they are referred to elsewhere as Shinto-ryu kenjutsu.

In addition to Shinto Muso-ryu jojutsu and Shinto-ryu kenjutsu, a number of separate arts are taught at various points in an exponent's training. They are considered assimilated arts, and include Uchida-ryu tanjojutsu, Ikkaku-ryu juttejutsu, Isshin-ryu kusarigamajutsu, and Ittatsu-ryu hojojutsu.

Sekiguchi Shinshin-ryu
関口新心流

Systems/weapons: jujutsu; kenjutsu/iaijutsu (odachi, kodachi)
Date founded: early Tokugawa period (ca. 1640)
Founder: Sekiguchi Yarokuemon Ujimune
Present representative: Sekiguchi Yoshio, 13th headmaster
Prefecture: Wakayama

Field notes: Sekiguchi Yarokuemon Ujimune was the descendant of hereditary retainers of the Imagawa family. His father was imprisoned upon their defeat during the Warring States period (1467-1568) and Ujimune had a difficult childhood. As a result, he resolved to excel in the martial arts to ensure his family's security. He traveled throughout Japan to study and improve his skill in combat, especially close-quarters grappling and arresting techniques.

The name of the *jujutsu* school that he subsequently founded, Sekiguchi Shinshin-ryu, is derived from the family name and Sekiguchi's belief that martial arts progress comes from daily training with a new (the first "shin" in the name) understanding (or spirit, *kokoro*, the second "shin"). Shinshin thus refers to a process of continually seeking new insights into the art's principles and techniques.

Sekiguchi Shinshin-ryu techniques utilize an opponent's power in a flowing manner. The Sekiguchi-ryu's basic assumption is that all combat, whether or not weapons are used, is decided by an ability in and understanding of grappling and the ability to defeat an enemy at close-quarters. As in many jujutsu traditions, the image of a willow tree is used to symbolize the principle of physical and mental flexibility of response; the willow can bend and withstand very heavy stress from snow or wind, then spring back to its original position after yielding to the initial onslaught without breaking.

At present, there are two separate lines of Sekiguchi-ryu; the other does not include the "Shinshin" in its name. Both practice *iai* and

Mutsuro Hiroyuki, having deflected his opponent's attack with a dagger, is temporarily immobilizing him before he counterattacks with his own weapon. 20th Kobudo Demonstration, Nippon Budokan, February 1997.

kenjutsu, but only the main line, still headed by a member of the Sekiguchi family, includes jujutsu. Grappling techniques are varied, from unarmed *yoroi kumiuchi* used on the battlefield to the unarmed self-defense common to peacetime, and also incorporates use of the long or short sword, or dagger, to defend against both empty-handed and weapons attacks. Sekiguchi-ryu exponents typically sit in a very wide stance, somewhere between a typical *seiza* (formal sitting posture) and *iaigoshi* (a kneeling posture used in sword-drawing techniques), as this position provides them with great stability and freedom of movement.

The iaijutsu techniques make frequent use of a movement called *tobi chigai,* where the exponent leaps into the air and reverses the position of his feet, using the power generated from the jump and the rotation of his hips to make a strong, decisive cut. Techniques are performed in all four directions, effectively giving a student a wide variety of responses to an attack. Sekiguchi-ryu *kiai* are long and sharp, and are

SWORD & SPIRIT

Seikguchi Yoshio performs an immobilizing technique before he strikes his opponent. 20th Kobudo Demonstration, Nippon Budokan, February 1997.

intended to help dominate the opponent and make the technique more effective. An unusual aspect of Sekiguchi-ryu swordsmanship is that power is concentrated in the right hand and the gripping action of the left hand is used to help stop the blade.

NEGISHI-RYU
根岸陽

Systems/weapons: shurikenjutsu (shuriken, tachi)
Date founded: late Tokugawa period (ca. 1870)
Founder: Negishi Shorei
Present representative: Saito Satoshi, 5th headmaster[2]
Prefecture: Tokyo

Field notes: This *shurikenjutsu* school was created after Negishi Shorei
had received all of the teachings of Gan-ryu, a comprehensive martial
arts system that included training in *tachiuchi* (swordsmanship), *iai*,
naginata, *kodachi*, *jo*, and *kumiuchi* (grappling), as well as *shuriken*. He
changed the shape and weight of the Gan-ryu-style weapon, making it
octagonal in cross-section and somewhat heavier, thus creating his own
style. Negishi-ryu does not use the four-, six-, or eight-pointed
shuriken known as *kurumaken* or *shaken*.

There are three basic methods for throwing shuriken in Negishi-ryu:
manji (named for the Buddhist swastika-like symbol), *toji*, and *jikishi*.
Each of these methods can be employed with a single, double, or triple
beat timing. The *manjikata* (throwing with the manji method) is the
most basic and is used to develop an understanding of proper timing,
distancing, and body movement. The *tojikata* and *jikishikata* are more
practical methods, to be used in actual combat, and are also called
shikakekata. Depending on whether the shuriken flies straight to the
target or rotates through a half-turn, the throwing technique is called
jikidaho or *hantendaho*.

There are a number of other applied techniques in the shikakekata:
mukiai (used when one is standing still); *torimai* (a technique used
while moving); *in-yo arasoi* (a technique for "rapid-fire" and for aiming

---

[2]See "Negishi-ryu Shurikenjutsu: An Interview with Saito Satoshi," page 89.

SWORD & SPIRIT

*Soke Saito Satoshi preparing to throw a shuriken
while holding his sword in jodan gamae. Nippon
Budokan, February 1997.*

at targets in front and back, or to the left and right); and an abstract, or non-physical, teaching called *shichi* (lit., "Four Knowledges," referring to the exponent's ability to correctly understand a situation, other people's intentions, the art's principles, and, in a more philosophic sense, the "Way" of the art).

Methods are also taught for using the shuriken in close-quarters combat and in conjunction with a sword, which is held in various positions (illustrated above), or sheathed and then drawn to complete a cut. Techniques for throwing while sitting or lying down and for unlighted conditions, when one is attacked at night, are also a part of the curriculum.

Kagita Chubei, on the left, thrusts at his opponent with a kama yari after deflecting the other spear upwards. 20th Kobudo Demonstration, Nippon Budokan, Tokyo, February 1997.

Hozoin-ryu Takada-ha
宝蔵院流高田派

Systems/weapons: sojutsu (su yari, kama yari)
Date founded: late Muromachi period (ca. 1560)
Founder: Hozoin Kakuzenbo In-ei
Present representative: Kagita Chubei
Prefecture: Nara

Field notes: The founder of Hozoin-ryu sojutsu, Hozoin Kakuzenbo In-ei, was a Buddhist priest of the Kofuku Temple in Nara. He studied swordsmanship under Kamiizumi Ise-no-kami Nobutsuna during the time when Yagyu Sekishusai Munetoshi, founder of Yagyu Shinkage-ryu hyoho was also training with Kamiizumi. Later, while traveling throughout Japan on *musha shugyo* to improve his skills, he met and trained with the famous spearman, Daizen Daifu Moritada. After further study and refining of the techniques and tactics of the *kama* (or *jumonji*) *yari*, he created Hozoin-ryu sojutsu. He transmitted the school's orthodox teachings to Nakamura Naomasa, one of his senior students, who created the Nakamura-ha of the Hozoin-ryu. Nakamura then passed on the most significant techniques and principles of spearmanship to Takada-ha founder, Takada Matabei Yoshitsugu. It is this line that continues to the present day.

Hozoin-ryu sojutsu techniques combine the thrusting movements common to the spear with a number of sophisticated offensive and defensive horizontal and vertical movements: *maki otoshi* (winding/rolling drop), *kiri otoshi* (cutting drop), *tataki otoshi* (striking drop), and *suri komi* (sliding and crowding). At present, exponents train against a yari, but in the past they also practiced against an opponent armed with a *tachi*, *naginata*, *su yari*, or *yumi*. At higher levels of training, single spearmen would train against multiple opponents.

Saito Satoshi was born in 1922, and has been training in karate and shurikenjutsu since his late teens. He worked as an official of the Tokyo Metropolitan Government in long-range planning and statistics, and retired as a department head. Since then he has taught planning and policy courses at the Tokyo Metropolitan University and has served as a special advisor on several governmental commissions and planning groups. He is headmaster of the Negishi-ryu and Yamamoto-ryu. This interview was conducted in Tokyo in late 1997, and was translated by Derek Steel.

Negishi-ryu Shurikenjutsu
An Interview with Saito Satoshi

Meik Skoss

Meik Skoss: Saito Sensei, I'd like to begin by asking you a little bit about your family and personal background.

Saito Satoshi Sensei: My father was a doctor and had little interest in bujutsu. He was so busy with his work that he had little time for that sort of thing, even if he had been interested. When he came home from work, he spent all his time reading German medical journals and such.

My paternal grandfather owned about sixty Japanese swords. During the Great Kanto Earthquake,[1] my father was able to rescue only about ten of them from the house before it burned. Had he truly been interested in the martial arts, I think he would have made an effort to save them all. Unfortunately, the other fifty or so were left behind and destroyed in the fires.

When did you take up martial arts?

As a student, back before the war, with Funakoshi Gichin Sensei at Keio University.

Did you practice in an actual karate dojo, or did your group borrow a kendo dojo or use some other space?

It was a genuine karate dojo, not a borrowed space. Actually, the room itself was divided into a boxing training area with a ring, and the karate dojo, which was just a bare wooden floor.

---

[1] On September 1, 1923 an earthquake and the fires in its aftermath destroyed over half of Tokyo.

The training involved both kata and pre-arranged sparring (yakusoku kumite)?

Yes. We also did freestyle sparring (*jiyu kumite*).

Freestyle sparring? Didn't Funakoshi Yoshitaka Sensei propose that later?

No. We were doing freestyle even under Gichin Sensei. From time to time, though, we would cross-train with the boxing students. Sometimes they'd bring their gloves over to our side or we'd go over to theirs. What we discovered was that, among people of more or less equal skill and experience, the boxers were usually stronger fighters. The reason for this is that boxers can execute many strikes and hand techniques quickly. On the other hand, this may well have been because we were wearing gloves. Although we never tried it, the results probably would have been different had we gone at it bare fisted. Without gloves, it is possible to down the opponent with a single blow. So I guess it would be more accurate to say that the boxers were stronger fighters when gloves were being worn. Like I said, although we never tried it, we karate men were confident that we would have been able to win in a bare-fisted fight.

Did karate at that time involve the use of throwing and pinning techniques?

No. We didn't practice that sort of thing. I should also say that we never did kicks with the top of the foot like they do now; we did them with the ball of the foot. We even did roundhouse kicks (*mawashigeri*) with the ball of the foot. Of course, we used the blade of the foot for sidekicks (*yokogeri*). Postwar karate has come to use the top of the foot for such kicks, the way they do in Thai kick-boxing. When Thai kick-boxing started to become more popular, doing roundhouses with the ball of the foot fell into disuse in Japanese karate.

These days, karate is widely viewed as a means of spiritual training. Would you say that the training back then, under Funakoshi Sensei, was more combat oriented?

Naturally it was, since it was expected that people were going to go off to fight in the war. The same was true with the kendo and *iaijutsu* we learned, which were taught based on the premise that these arts might be used on the battlefield. Of course, they included many techniques that have been banned today. This is quite different from students these days, who pursue such arts as sports.

When did you start learning shurikenjutsu?

During my university preparatory course, which was part of the old education system. Back then, college education was divided into a preparatory course, a regular course, graduate school, and so on. I started studying karate during the first year of my preparatory course. My older brother was also a Keio student and had done karate, so it was natural for me to follow in his footsteps. He told me about a Negishi-ryu shuriken teacher by the name of Naruse Kanji, so the two of us went together to see him.[2]

What form does training in Negishi-ryu take?

Naturally we begin with easier skills and ways of throwing. For example, we have a straight, direct throw (*jikidaho*), without the *shuriken* making any turns. Students begin practicing this at about three meters, using a shuriken that is somewhat cylindrical. Once students can do it at three meters, the distance is increased, and they start using a different kind of shuriken, like the triangular type Pierre and his wife use.[3] Cylindrical shuriken have an effective range of only about six meters, even using jikidaho. For distances greater than that, you have to use a

---

[2] See "Field Guide to the Japanese Classical Martial Arts," page 84 for more background on this school.

[3] Pierre and Claire Simon, students of Saito Sensei, now live and teach in Toulouse, France.

different type of shuriken. It is also necessary to integrate a half turn (*hanten*) of the shuriken into the throw.

Later, if students stay with it, they are taught targeting methods and other secrets, the characteristics of other shuriken styles, and about the contents of the *densho* (transmission scrolls) of Negishi-ryu and other styles. I have made a point of collecting as much material as possible.

Incidentally, I would like to publish a book on shuriken sometime, for which I have collected quite a bit of material, including photographs. However, I have so many things to do these days that I never seem to get time to work on it. On the other hand, I think I'd better start soon, because it would really be a shame if I died without writing it all down.

What is the range of the shaken, the throwing-star-type shuriken?

Pretty much as far as your arm strength allows you to throw it. On the other hand, the shaken's accuracy is extremely poor. For example, such a shuriken is easily affected by any kind of crosswind. Of course, an ordinary spike-type shuriken is affected to some degree, but shaken are particularly susceptible to wind. For example, that happened once when I was demonstrating at the Hibiya Public Hall.

Actually, you understand this much better if you practice outside in a field instead of in an enclosed dojo. I used to practice outside all the time. Anyway, when there is a tailwind influencing your shuriken, you have to throw it as if the target was somewhat closer than it actually is. The opposite is true in the case of a headwind: you have to throw the blade as if the target was somewhat further away than it actually is. In any case, although a shuriken is a relatively heavy piece of iron, it is still greatly influenced by wind, and the shaken is even more susceptible. In fact, even when there is no wind, it is actually quite difficult to get the shaken to fly in the way you intend.

Juji shaken (cross-shaped, with four points) often bounce off the target. This is mainly because any two adjacent spikes form an isosceles triangle, with the large flat line between the points of the spikes having a greater chance of hitting the target than the points of the spikes themselves. The most effective shaken is the *happo* (eight-pointed) type.

How deep do such shaken penetrate? Two or three centimeters at the most?

Hardly at all if the person is wearing clothes, particularly if they are wearing several layers. For that reason, the primary targets are the face or the back of the hand, and also the legs and feet. During demonstrations, we throw at a point on the target about the height of our own face. Actually, though, it is also essential to practice targeting around the area of the navel, because this is the level of the hands of an opponent wielding a sword. It is important to practice targeting the hands because this was one of the most effective ways to inflict meaningful damage. Back in the days when people still fought with swords, this was considered top secret information. You can put it in your book now, if you want [laughs].

Of course, this is not to say that the face cannot also be a target, but the ideal in using a shuriken is to deprive your opponent of his capacity to fight, and thereby force him to give in or yield without having to resort to fighting with swords. If that fails, if you hit his hand with your shuriken but he still insists on coming after you, then, of course, you have to resort to using your sword to cut him down. In this way, using shurikenjutsu involves what is called a two-level strategy (*nidangamae*).

People in Japan used to dress their upper bodies in fairly thick layers, but wore only in relatively thin *hakama* on their lower bodies and legs. In *suhada kenjutsu* (unarmored swordsmanship, or swordsmanship in normal, Japanese-style clothing), this part around the thigh would be quite a bit thinner, so that was also a target. In this connection, I would also mention Yasuda Zenjiro, a master of Otsuki-ryu kenjutsu from Hiroshima, who died at the age of ninety-one. I used to make a point of visiting him in Hiroshima every year and pay him my respects on my way back from Hakata, where I go for a memorial service for my wartime comrades.

Yasuda Sensei's teacher, Okamoto Muneshige, lived during the end of the Edo period, in the so-called *bakumatsu* period. He was a samurai from the Aizu feudal domain who was employed in Kyoto as part of the shogunate's security force, along with Kondo Isamu and Hijikata Toshizo of the Shinsengumi. He was responsible for arresting master-less samurai from the Tenno-ha.[4] Because of that, he became a target for assassination by imperial loyalists. There were about three attempts on his life in which he was suddenly attacked by assassins.

Yasuda Sensei told me these stories. He also talked about the various types of kenjutsu training and conditions that he experienced under Okamoto Sensei. He wrote it all down over the years, giving these writings to me. One of these stories tells about one of these assassination attempts, in which Okamoto was attacked by five imperial loyalists. One had a *teyari* (short spear) that was about five or six *shaku*[5] long; the other four had swords. Thinking quickly, Okamoto Sensei realized that the man with the spear was the most dangerous and that he would need to deal with him first. So he deliberately sliced his sword strongly into the haft of the man's spear, so deeply that it became embedded. This allowed him to momentarily immobilize the spear, during which time he cut the man with his *wakizashi* (short sword). Then he used this short sword, which was a relatively longer one of about one shaku eight *sun*, to deal with the other four. Incidentally, warriors truly concerned with being able to fight would generally choose a slightly long-ish wakizashi as a companion to their *katana* because they knew they might have to actually rely on it. Therefore, they felt more comfortable with a longer one.

Anyway, Okamoto used his wakizashi to cut down three of the remaining attackers. The fifth one fled after seeing his companions sprawled on the ground. However, as this last man ran, he felt a sharp

[4] Bakumatsu is a term used to describe the final days of the Tokugawa shogunate, about 1853-1867; the Shinsengumi was a group of pro-shogunate warriors hired by the Tokugawa government to suppress dissent; the Tenno-ha was the imperial loyalist faction, which supported the restoration of the emperor and the overthrow of the Tokugawa shogunate.

[5] A shaku is a unit of length about 30.3 centimeters, or 11.9 inches. Shaku are divided into ten *sun*. Japanese swords are still measured using these units.

pain in his thigh and gradually he couldn't move it very well. When he looked down, he found he had been hit in the thigh by two shuriken and was bleeding profusely. He realized that, if he had stayed to fight any longer, he probably would have been done in like his companions. So, Otsuki-ryu practitioners also use shuriken, of which they always carried a dozen or so. However, Okamoto did not use them as his main weapon in that particular encounter.

Where were those twelve shuriken carried?

There weren't necessarily twelve. That was just Okamoto Sensei's preference. He carried three or four in his *koshiita* (the back stay of a man's hakama) and the rest in a leather bag inside his kimono. During the fight I described above, though, he was too busy dealing with the spear to think of using them. He was probably worried that his opponents might use shuriken on him. One of the things he told Yasuda Sensei was that it was necessary to practice not only throwing shuriken, but also how to avoid or defend against them. Okamoto Muneshige passed on to Yasuda Sensei this sort of important information that he had learned from experience. For example, a shuriken, even a thin one, planted in a man's thigh will prevent him from being able to continue fighting. Also, the best way to defend against a shuriken is to be able to perceive which of your opponents is preparing to use one and make dispatching that man your priority, just as Okamoto perceived the attacker with the spear as the most dangerous and dealt with him first. People were very concerned with these things back then.

Attention to such details seems relevant to combat even today, and is also an important part of keeping the shuriken tradition alive today, don't you think?

In fact, of late, the American Special Forces and other military units are very interested in Japanese shuriken. One reason is that you can kill an opponent by covering the shuriken with a poison like wolfsbane or aconite. Shuriken are also useful for survival outdoors, for example, by people engaged in infiltration and spying or intelligence activities in enemy territory, who have to live out in the woods for months at a time. They can't very well carry all the food they'll need for that time, and the empty cans or trash might give away their presence to the enemy. So, shuriken are good for procuring food because they are easily portable and can be used to hunt small game quietly. With the addition of poison, you could probably even hunt slightly larger animals like small deer. Thicker-skinned animals like boar would be impossible, of course. The Ainu used to use poisoned arrows to kill bears, but the shuriken does not have a mechanism to propel it, so there is an upper limit to its effectiveness. Anyway, I have received calls from people in the United States who are interested in having me teach this sort of thing.

I reply that there are various conditions they have to meet if I am going to teach them. For one, there is not much housing space in Japan, with everyone living in so-called rabbit hutches. However, the fact is, unless you have space to practice at home, you will not progress. So you really need your own house, with enough space to throw a shuriken in, preferably with some land around it. A garden or something like that would do. In any case, you have to have a place you can practice without accidentally harming or annoying your neighbors.

How many students do you have presently?
There is Mr. Tomabechi, whom I have selected as my successor, and there are two individuals from Chiba. There is also an individual from the Self-Defense Forces. He was transferred to Hokkaido and does not come often now, although he still practices. In fact, he has fashioned a sort of shuriken holster for himself to carry about ten triangular cross-section shuriken.

I also have some older students. One is an American, who now lives in Hawaii. He originally wanted to learn shuriken for self-defense purposes. I told him that a pistol would probably be better for that, and I think he and his wife now practice that, too.

There is a baseball player, a pitcher for the Yomiuri Giants. He trained with me for about three years so that he could improve his ability to throw a certain kind of pitch.

One student comes from Croatia. He is an army cartographer. He is a very fine man and very good at drafting. He was introduced to me by a man from Miyazaki Prefecture who is deeply involved in martial arts research. My Croatian student is very enthusiastic and has tried to design his own shuriken, which I then corrected.

Actually, the suitability of a particular shuriken for long- or short-range throwing depends on its center of gravity. Those sorts of techniques need to be practiced, of course. However, a middle-range shuriken is most convenient.

Anyway, my Croatian student took a number of measurements of the various types and made his own. He did very good work. Normally, shuriken are wrapped with paper and string, then covered in a coat of lacquer. Lacquer is very hard to work with, so people use wood glue and paper in layers. The Croatian man tried to use golf club tape, but that is not as good.

I think that practicing only shurikenjutsu is insufficient. It is something one should do after one has developed proficiency in another martial art. Also, shuriken is something many people want to do just because it seems interesting. However, people who do it for this reason tend not to last long and quit after a while. People may also misuse it for evil purposes. So I think it is best if someone has relatively extensive experience in some other martial art, be it karate, kendo, jodo, or whatever. For that reason, I require anyone who is to become my student to have first done some other martial art.

You learned shuriken from both Naruse Sensei and Maeda Sensei?

No, just Naruse Sensei. Maeda Isamu Sensei and I were contemporaries under Naruse Sensei. The headmastership (*soke*) was passed to me from Maeda Sensei because he felt that his shuriken technique was too idiosyncratic and imbued with too much *garyu* (personal style) to be considered pure Negishi-ryu. I have some letters from Maeda Sensei in which he talks about how he felt his own style was too quirky, as if it were mixed with some other style. His throw is quite unlike how it is done in Negishi-ryu. Also, I received instruction under Naruse Sensei for a relatively longer time than Maeda Sensei did. Then I went into

Saito Satoshi demonstrating the jikihado method of throwing the shuriken. 20th Kobudo Demonstration, Nippon Budokan, February 1997.

the military to become an officer candidate. Due to the war, Naruse Sensei did not know what would happen to Japan or to himself. However, he knew that he wanted to leave his shurikenjutsu and iaijutsu for future generations by passing it on to a successor. If Japan was defeated or destroyed, he knew that he might be defeated or destroyed with it. He had one of the katana he had owned for a long time equipped with military sword fittings so that I could take it with me. When I was in the flying corps in Hamamatsu, he told me that he wanted to give me his shurikenjutsu and iaijutsu and he wanted me to be his successor in these arts.

So Maeda Sensei was the headmaster for a time?

Yes, but it's like this: the only students of Naruse Sensei who survived the war are myself, Maeda Sensei, and Mr. Shirakami. Maeda Sensei was the eldest, so the position of headmaster was passed to him first, with the understanding that he would later pass it to me, which he did on January 1, in 1959. Also, most of Naruse Sensei's surviving family members are women. The eldest daughter's name is Eiko. Maeda Sensei sent a letter to her in 1959 informing her that the soke position was to be transferred to Tokyo.

Naruse Sensei died in 1948. He was fond of his liquor, especially *shochu*, which he had heated and drank while sitting under the *kotatsu* in the winter. This eventually did him in, as he developed cirrhosis of the liver or some kind of liver cancer. After he passed away, the three of us — Mr. Maeda, Mr. Shirakami, and I — talked about it. We decided that, since Mr. Maeda was the oldest, about ten years older than I was, he should become the headmaster, at least for the time being, and later pass it on to me in Tokyo. In fact, however, Naruse Sensei had already advised me that I was to be his successor, but in any case, that was how we did it. Maeda Sensei sent a letter in 1959, as I mentioned, to Naruse Sensei's eldest daughter, Eiko. She responded with a letter indicating her approval. That concluded the formal transfer of the soke position to me.

Was there any special ceremony held?
No, nothing in particular, just the letter indicating her consent to the transfer.

So, Naruse Sensei was the soke of both Negishi-ryu and Yamamoto-ryu?
That's right. He was also involved in the resurrection of Shirai-ryu shurikenjutsu, which had been lost. On the other hand, Negishi-ryu has been handed down continuously.

However, here is something strange: for some reason, Negishi-ryu is not passed on by *isshi soden* (the formal transmission from father to son, generally through the eldest son). To put it in other words, Negishi-ryu has not been transmitted by blood or familial ties. Rather, it has been simply handed down from teacher to student and from that student to his students.

The founder of the style was named Negishi Shorei. He was from Gumma Prefecture. There is an interesting story about when he went off to the front in the Russo-Japanese War. Apparently, he slung a great big sword over his shoulder and marched valiantly off to war, to the vigorous cheers of all those around. In other words, it was a rather ostentatious departure. He was an officer, of course, a first lieutenant in the army. However, when the war was over and the Japanese forces were returning in triumph, he went to America. According to some rumors, when the supposedly valiant Negishi Shorei actually faced the hail of bullets on the battlefield, he hid behind a big tree and shook like a leaf! I do not know if this is true, mind you, but the story spread. In any case, he was unable to continue living in Japan, presumably due to the shame involved, so he set out for America.

Negishi Shorei's grandson now lives here in Tokyo, in Setagaya Ward. I sent a letter to him saying that I would like to meet and talk with him since he was a descendant of Negishi Shorei. Then I called him on the telephone. His wife answered and, when I explained my intentions, she told me that her husband no longer had anything to do with Negishi-ryu or shurikenjutsu, and for that reason would prefer that we didn't meet. The same is true of Naruse Sensei's son, who did not succeed his father, either. As for me, I also do not have any children. So for some reason — perhaps it is just fate — Negishi-ryu does not have a tradition of succession by blood or kinship. The successor I have chosen is Tomabechi Yoshimi. He is also a senior student of Daito-ryu aikijujutsu.

Have you ever practiced any of the modern budo?
In the military I had to do kendo, but not the sort we have today. Military kendo involved cutting at the legs, thrusting at the torso, throwing, and so on. Thrusting at the abdomen is actually one of the best techniques. However, they went and made all sorts of rules; for example, now you can only thrust to the throat. With that, kendo became a non-combative martial art.

I also did *jukendo* when I was a student. One of the biggest differences in the Japanese way of teaching bayonet fighting is that they taught it using protective armor, while the American military trains without such safety gear.

What do you think of modern budo?

I think that many modern sports evolved from combat or competition between individuals. That evolution into sports saw the increasing addition of rules, and it is these rules that have made modern budo into sports. Truly combative budo have no rules. The fewer the rules, the more combative the bujutsu. People like myself, who work with truly combative bujutsu, essentially have no interest in such sportified versions. Of course, if there are not too many rules, and the techniques used can be easily switched into more combative mode, then this is not so far off from old-style or *koryu bujutsu* and there may be a need to study such things.

Do you think there is any value in matches or competition?

Matches are conducted based on various predetermined rules. For example, in karate, if you decide that all attacks will be stopped short of the actual target, given the application of *sundome* (stopping the blow one sun away from the target), then this is not very combative at all, is it? Once, when I was teaching karate, I noticed that when sundome is used, people start to neglect defending their face adequately. When I was teaching, we used to use a catcher's mask as a face protector, and the thinnest protective gloves we could find, which turned out to be kendo *kote*. We also used a kendo chest protector (*do*) to protect the midsection, without which it really hurts to get hit by a kendo glove. Boxing gloves are double-layered and can be avoided or blocked fairly easily, but kendo kote are thinner and can sneak through smaller openings, so we decided to use those. It was as close as we could get to bare fists, while still having some protection. Then, since it hurts to get hit full bore in the head, even with the mask, we restricted punching to only about twenty percent of full force, and practiced in three-minute bouts followed by one-minute rest periods. In this way, we added a lot of rules to our practice. Using this equipment, when students got hit in the head for real, the blow would stimulate them to think about ways they might start protecting that area a little better. In other words, it added a little reality to the experience. When they used only sundome techniques, they did not think about protecting their faces much, because they knew the punches would not really have much effect. Getting hit for real, though, even with the protective equipment, made students realize what they really needed to be doing.

I recall seeing a recent karate bout in which a senior teacher was awarded a point for executing a backfist strike (uraken) while he was leaping through the air. I suppose that he did make contact with his opponent, but I cannot imagine such a strike would do much damage if it were for real.

I doubt it, too. One thing I learned from Fujita Sensei of the Koga-ryu was that, while the regular front punch (*seiken*) is important, one of the most effective strikes is done with the second knuckle of the middle finger raised, the *nakadaka ipponken*. The thing is, it really hurts your knuckle unless you have conditioned it. If you can do this strike, though, you can down even the strongest man, totally knocking the wind out of him, with one blow to certain parts of the chest. You can dent a man's skull with it.

Tell us a little about your training and how it related to your military service.

Students in my day were more or less expected to join the military. In battle, of course, they would be using rifles and artillery, but, failing those, it was expected that they would fight with their *gunto* (military-issue swords). If those broke, they would be expected to engage in hand-to-hand combat. My shuriken and iai teachers told me that if I became an officer, I should practice iaijutsu using a real sword, instead of kendo. They felt that it would be a waste of time to practice waving a *shinai* (bamboo practice sword) around like they do in kendo, and that I would never learn to cut anyone properly doing that. So I practiced iaijutsu. In case it came to fighting with my bare hands, I learned karate from Funakoshi Gichin Sensei.

After the war, I went to Fujita Seiko Sensei, a famous exponent of Koga-ryu ninjutsu, and learned various things about how to use the fan (*sensu*). As it turned out, this included some of the same principles that I had learned during the war about firing artillery, such as surveying and using a transit to measure the distance relating to the enemy's position. The measurement was different in the artillery in that we used meters as the unit of measure, while ninjutsu surveying techniques use *ken* (the length of two standard *tatami* mats). The ninjutsu fan can be opened to 180 degrees and serves as a kind of protractor. The number of spines on the fan was a style secret, which they would describe using vague phrases such as, "like the number of holes in a lotus root." This ambiguous description was typical of Japanese martial arts: they did not teach in a straightforward way.

So, the number of spines in the Koga-ryu fan was described as "like the holes in the lotus root." As a result, the teaching was impenetrable to outsiders. After all, if you cut a lotus root and count the holes, some will have seven, some twelve, and so on. A statistical analysis of the number of holes in a lotus root will yield the number nine, which is the number of spines in the *ninja* fan. So the ninjutsu fan, which was used as a measuring device, had nine spines, which were used to generate a system of trigonometric functions, including sines and cosines. As a bujutsu, it was quite well thought out and not arbitrary at all, with stratagems based solidly in mathematics and science.

Such thinking was not limited to ninjutsu, of course. For example, there is a Japanese system of mathematical calculation called Seki-ryu wasan, founded by Seki Takakazu. It included differential and integral calculus and had calculated the value of *pi* to several tens of decimal places. So you see, knowledge of such advanced mathematics was not limited just to Koga-ryu ninjutsu. There have always been people who have been aware of it. However, one of the reasons that this awareness was not more widespread during the Edo period, when Seki-ryu was developed, was that, as in bujutsu, its practitioners were given to keeping such things secret, as a kind of esotericism. Only certain people were aware of the formulae or recipes.

What was your major in university?
I studied law. Originally, I intended to become a lawyer or public prosecutor. However, because of the war, the majority of people pursuing such cultural majors were drafted into the student army. So I was

SWORD & SPIRIT

obliged to serve in the military beginning in 1943. By the time I was discharged, of course, Japan was in shambles. So it was not really possible for me to settle back into my studies. Instead, I took various part-time jobs, for example handling and transporting wares to be sold on the postwar black market. Inflation was so bad that my family simply could not make ends meet on my father's salary. We couldn't eat. I also took jobs as a private tutor. Studying law required a more stable environment than was possible at the time, especially given all the preparation you need to do for the various exams. As it turned out, I ended up passing the test to become an administrative assistant in the Tokyo Metropolitan Office. I started out in the statistics department, then moved to the planning department. Then, to enter the manager class, I had to pass a manager's exam.

What did you do during your military service?

I trained as an artillery officer and aircraft navigator. In the end, I was stationed with the Western Army in Fukuoka, Kyushu, where I was responsible for overseeing military operations in the regions surrounding Kyushu and Shikoku, as well as Amami Oshima, Okinawa, and so on. I was in the strategy room, where we gathered information on what was happening on the battlefields, including the reports of the fierce battles being waged and the honorable deaths by *kamikaze* pilots as the Japanese there fought to the bitter end. The kamikaze were somewhat effective at first. However, the American forces eventually applied mathematical and scientific methods to devise strategies to prevent attacks from succeeding. In Japan, however, when we heard the signal indicating an attack had occurred, we would automatically count it as a hit and assume that damage had been done to the intended target. If there were ten different signals — the pilots would press a button in their planes to sound a buzzer at the headquarters — we would calculate the effects of these attacks as, say, strikes on five battleships, two cruisers, and three carriers. But it really was only guesswork, and based on this sort of mistaken information, Japanese strategy was also in error.

This shows how important information is. Are you familiar with the field of operations research? For example, it is common for private corporations to conduct scientific calculations using statistics and other mathematics. This has been in use for a long time in sampling theory, for example. The various operations research methods used by the American military during the war came to be employed by private corporations after the war, in production management and quality control, to prevent the production of defective products.

During the war, the American military used operations research to learn how to handle kamikaze attacks. They gathered and examined the data of all the experiences they'd had with kamikaze up to that point. As a result, they told any ships larger than a cruiser to circle around and around if faced with a kamikaze attack. Smaller ships like destroyers were told to move in a straight line. They studied all of this using the mathematical methods and techniques of operations research. The orders came from the people at the top. The goal was to determine from the outset how best to minimize Allied losses and damage. You have heard of game theory, haven't you? Do you do A or B, do you go this way or that way? Based on what your enemy does and on what you and your allies have, you determine what options you should or should not pursue. Operations research is a form of strategic analysis.

Japan had no knowledge of game theory, so the commanders made their decisions on where to send their ships not on any scientific basis, but merely on, say, which way had the better weather or where they thought the American fleet was arrayed. The Americans would then dispatch reconnaissance planes to determine how the Japanese fleet was arrayed and what course they had chosen. Based on this information, they would point their ships in whatever direction they needed to intercept or outflank us.

The Japanese forces had no knowledge of the game theory the Americans were using. If they had, they would have been able to predict what methods the American fleet intended to use. But they did not. So, the American planes sank about ninety percent of our cargo ships and tankers, one after another. The troops on board could swim to safety, but the important artillery, tanks, and ammunition were all lost. The most important, perhaps, was the loss of ammunition. You cannot fight a war without ammunition.

So the moral of this story seems to be that you have to understand what sort of means, methods, or ways of thinking the enemy has at its disposal and factor these into your own strategy. If I might change the subject slightly: in one sense, you pursue Negishi-ryu as a sort of cultural preservation, but is there any other reason you train in the koryu bujutsu?

One reason might be that the koryu bujutsu embody the *kokorogamae* (traditional mental stance) of the Japanese people, which is something I do not want to be forgotten. I think the classical martial arts embody a certain bravery, an unwillingness to be defeated, that characterized the Japanese people in the past. For this reason, I think we must continue to practice and teach koryu bujutsu. We do not want to lose our traditional spirit and become strange and unnatural Japanese. The classical martial arts were one of the significant foundations of traditional Japan. For example, they have influenced the language itself. We still use expressions like *shinogi wo kezuru* (to fight furiously, to be involved in fierce competition), *saya ate* (to be rivals), and *seppa ga tsumaru* (to be driven into a tight corner or to be compelled by necessity, referring to the tightness of the spacers on sword fittings). There are quite a few of these terms in the Japanese language that come from koryu bujutsu.

The koryu bujutsu have also had a significant influence on the Japanese cultural traditions that are now depicted in *kabuki* and Noh plays and period dramas on television. So it is important for people to do these things and teach them to others, especially their psychological and spiritual aspects. For if we lose knowledge of the reality of these traditions, then we will eventually lose our identity as Japanese.

Unfortunately, many Japanese people today do not even think about such things. They think that as long as Japan is a peaceful country foreign enemies will never attack us, so we do not have to be prepared for such things. This may be only what people say up front, their *tatemae*; but in any case, there are many who think this way, even in the education system. However, if the feeling that we must protect our nation and culture drops to zero, then I think we are no longer Japanese. I suppose foreigners like yourselves have wondered, for example, about the psychological and spiritual makeup of the Japanese. Understanding what makes the Japanese, or any people, tick is one thing that will help us get along together in the world.

Another reason to practice koryu bujutsu is to train oneself to ride out or cut one's way out of adversity and bad situations. It contains methods to cultivate the courage needed to face such difficulties. At the basis of this is the idea of being able to sacrifice oneself (*sutemi no kokoro*) if that is what is necessary. This can apply to other aspects of life. For example, when you are employed at or running a company, or when negotiating with others, or when you have failed, made a mistake, or otherwise done something damaging to your company, you have to be able to resign, or do whatever is necessary, and have the courage to take responsibility. This sort of personal responsibility will probably become even more important henceforth, given the drastic changes taking place in the Japanese business and economic spheres these days.

At its ultimate extreme, koryu bujutsu involves *sutemi* (sacrifice). If you think for a moment about saving your own life, or that your own life is precious, you will not be able to engage in *shinken shobu* (real combat; literally, combat with live swords). Or you will be cut down or otherwise defeated. However, you may well find circumstances in which you will have to fight, to defend yourself, your honor, your family, your status, your fortune. You have to be prepared to sacrifice yourself and cut your own way out of such situations.

In all the martial arts, including karate and kenjutsu, we practice concentrating one's gaze on a specific point (*metsuke*). Depending on the *ryuha*, there are various teachings about metsuke. For example, looking at the tip of the opponent's nose or their sword-hand or whatever. However, I think looking at one of their eyes is the most effective. You can perceive your opponent's movements and intentions. You can tell where they are going to attack or strike. I have used this in karate kumite. My opponent asked me how I avoided his strikes. I said that he kept looking at the place he was going to strike before he did so. He

SWORD & SPIRIT

said he certainly was not doing such a thing, but in fact one of his eyes always moved to that spot, if only for an instant, before he struck. He just was not conscious of doing it. Even fourth- and fifth-dan level people do this. This is the sort of training that is impossible to get with kata training alone. You have to do some sort of free-style training, like *randori* in judo or kumite in karate, in which you are really going for it.

In Yagyu Shinkage-ryu, you look at the opponent's sword-bearing hand. For me, I look at my opponent's right eye, the one on the left from my perspective. This is how we do it in Negishi-ryu. If you keep looking from eye to eye, your opponent will get the sense that you are agitated or otherwise unstable. I have used this koryu bujutsu technique when I had to deal with Japanese gangsters when I was working in the Tokyo Metropolitan Office. It gives your opponent a very strange and uneasy feeling if your eyes are not moving at all as you gaze at him. It shows a certain intention on your part. I used this when negotiating with the *oyabun* (bosses) of gangs, when they came to surround me. This goes back to the spirit of sutemi I talked about earlier, a spirit of demonstrating a willingness to have things end in *aiuchi* (where both opponents mutually kill or strike each other down) if that is necessary. It is a spirit that you will not be defeated; that you will take your opponent down, no matter what the cost; that even if he wants to kill you, he will not be able to do it simply. These things you can convey through metsuke. I have used this to convey my intentions, attitude, or spirit in numerous potentially dangerous situations, and it has served me well. One of the great things about koryu bujutsu is that they contain useful teachings that have broader application. Even a single teaching you receive from your teacher can have very extensive implications.

*Liam Keeley joined the Tatsumi-ryu in 1984; he has been awarded mokuroku for iai, kenjutsu, and yawara. He is the book review columnist for **Martial Arts Illustrated**, and is a member of the board of directors of the International Hoplology Society.*

THE TOJUTSU OF THE TATSUMI-RYU,
MURPHY'S LAW, AND THE K.I.S.S. PRINCIPLE

Liam Keeley

When I returned to Japan for the third time in 1984, I was deter-mined to enter a traditional school of martial arts, more particularly one that was sword-based, to fulfill my emic requirements as a would-be hoplologist.[1] I was lucky enough to be accepted into the Tatsumi-ryu, a *koryu* that predates the Tokugawa shogunate (1603-1867). Since I had previously trained in a variety of combative arts, I found I was able to handle the physical challenge of learning a new art relatively easily, but my preconceptions about the structure of the system were being continually challenged. In a sense, this article is a summary of my musings on the nature of combative systems, based particularly on my experiences with the Tatsumi-ryu, together with some long rambling conversations with kindred spirits, over the last fourteen years.

Tatsumi-ryu iai has a number of features that are in contrast to the general image of *iai*: basic practice is done while walking; there is a very distinctive draw; there are only two central techniques from which all variations come; the curriculum is based on a three-level training

---

[1] Hoplology is the study of human combative behavior. According to hoplologists, who borrowed the terms from cultural anthropology, emic refers to someone who participates in the activities being described, studied, or analyzed, while etic refers to an "outsider."

program (*jo*, *ha*, *kyu*); techniques are economical; the number of techniques is limited; and there is a very high degree of integration between the iai, or solo sword-drawing, and the *kenjutsu*, practiced in pairs. I had originally intended to limit the discussion of Tatsumi-ryu technique to the iai component, but the more I thought and wrote about it, the harder it became to consider the iai in isolation from the rest of the Tatsumi-ryu syllabus. This article then, will deal with Tatsumi-ryu *tojutsu*, a term that includes both iai and kenjutsu as a coherent system. I say "iai" as opposed to "*iaijutsu*" deliberately, as in the earliest documents of the Tatsumi-ryu the *-jutsu* suffix was not used; this is the term members of the *ryu* tend to use today.

Modern iaido practitioners are frequently confronted by questions: "Just how realistic are the moves from the point of view of combat? Isn't paired practice, such as in kenjutsu, more viable and more closely related to a true system of combat? What was the place of solo practice in the Japanese warrior's training regimen?" Hunter B. Armstrong outlined some prevailing misconceptions in his chapter "The Koryu Bujutsu Experience," in the first volume of this series. I'd like to look more closely at iai or solo sword-drawing as it exists within a classical Japanese combat system.

In general, I would say that the modern tendency in the martial arts is to look at a system's effectiveness from the viewpoint of the practitioner. However, I would like to look at the system qua system, both at how the system is designed and at what the system is designed to do, rather than what an individual can do with the system. The individual and the system may, in fact, have very different priorities and even goals. To give just one modern example, Colonel Jeff Cooper, doyen of modern pistol shooting, concluded in his article "Combat Handguns" that, while from the point of view of the Army, it was probably not worth equipping each soldier with a pistol, the number of lives thus saved being negligible, the point of view of the soldier, who by carrying a pistol could possibly save his life, was quite different. In the Japanese context, while a student may aspire to being a master swordsman, the ryu, depending on the situation, and particularly in time of war, may be more interested in producing a number of reasonably competent swordsmen in as short a space of time as possible.[2] Let me put this in modern terms: the primary object of a combatives instructor is not to produce other combat instructors (although such specialized courses obviously exist), but to produce more combatively effective soldiers.

How did the Japanese traditions accomplish these goals? How did different types of training contribute to a warrior's overall efficiency? Before we can answer these questions we need to understand exactly what constitutes an effective combat system. Then we can examine the Tatsumi-ryu tojutsu in light of these understandings, and see to what extent iai fulfills the needs of combat training in an actual system that was used on the battlefield.

In my opinion, the desirable qualities of a combatively effective system are efficiency of technique; economy of technique — all extraneous movement[3] is abhorred; parsimony of technique — the absolute number of techniques is carefully limited; and a very high degree of integration of techniques within the system.

Techniques to be used in combat must be both biomechanically efficient and behaviorally appropriate. It is important not to overlook this latter. Looked at only from the viewpoint of biomechanics, a movement may be efficient, but it might not be combatively efficient, i.e. effective. When my daughter Rina was about six, she advised me that the way to deal with monsters was to chop their heads off, and then punch them in the stomach. While the punch might be biomechanically faultless, it is neither efficient nor appropriate behavior. It is, I think, a good example of "overkill." Combative parameters may dictate that movements are actually not as biomechanically efficient as they could be,

---

[2] Ellis Amdur, a practitioner of Araki-ryu, told me, "In the Araki-ryu, there is a book my teacher once showed me which listed the times taken to attain *menkyo kaiden*. In the peace time bracketing the Meiji period and the wars with Russia and China, it took approximately twelve to fourteen years. During wartime, two guys got menkyo kaiden in five and seven years."

[3] Chiba Shusaku (1794-1855) as quoted in Draeger: "1) Silence: move any time, any place, in any efficient manner, but without making noise. 2) Walk: take whatever number of steps the situation requires, but do so in a natural manner…" (84).

because of other factors, such as the necessity to keep yourself covered, etc. This fits in with Draeger's argument that combative behavior is essentially conservative.

A combat-oriented system also requires simplicity of movement, in other words, economy of technique. The time-honored philosophical concept, Occam's Razor, "Entities ought not be multiplied needlessly," describes parsimony of technique. Just as each single technique should be stripped of extraneous movements, it is logical, from the points of view of both teaching and learning, that techniques should be kept to the minimum. Better to have only a few techniques that always work than dozens that only sometimes work, or only work in part. The old drill instructor adage, "Keep It Short and Simple" (the so-called K.I.S.S. principle) is an apt description of this quality.

This also applies to the length of the sequences taught. It is highly unlikely that long and complicated sequences will be retained in stressful situations such as combat.[4] Just as a chain is only as strong as its weakest link, long "necessary" sequences are easily betrayed by weak techniques. By their very nature, they are prone to disruption; and the longer the sequence, the more easily they can be disrupted. Murphy's Law applies just as much to the martial arts as it does to any other field of human endeavor: "If something can go wrong, it will."

The final element of combative effectiveness, integration of technique, incorporates biomechanics, transferable skills, and mindset. Basic techniques should not only be biomechanically efficient, involving major muscle groups and, wherever possible, eschewing techniques

---

[4] Here we need to distinguish between "necessary" and "unnecessary." There are some styles that use relatively long sequences as a training device. On closer examination, these long sequences turn out to be technically "unnecessary," i.e. they are composed of shorter "necessary" sequences, which are actually complete in themselves. One thinks of *kata* such as the *enpi* of the Yagyu Shinkage-ryu, which is made up of half a dozen shorter sequences, and I understand the Katori Shinto-ryu has a similar approach. What I am criticizing are long "necessary" sequences, in which all the movements in the sequence are required to achieve the technique's goal. To clear this up, it may help you to repeat three times, "Long 'necessary' sequences are unnecessary. Long 'necessary' sequences are unnecessary. Long...." I am indebted to Ellis Amdur for this terminology.

SWORD & SPIRIT

dependent on fine motor skills, but must also be transferable, i.e. there should be substantial carry-over in that both the same physical techniques can be done with different weapons and that incoming attacks by different weapons can be dealt with using the same techniques. Moreover, the techniques themselves need to be sufficiently flexible to be able to be used effectively by a wide range of body types.[5] Mindset implies that even if the weapon used by the warrior changes, his basic mindset should be the same. A different weapon does not require an entirely different approach. What I have to say regarding mindset can be summed up in Hunter Armstrong's memorable phrase, "One mind, any weapon."[6]

This category also includes "intra-technique" integration. By this I mean that the system's techniques must be constructed in such a fashion that the exponent is never at a loss, never left out on a limb, as it were. I am thinking here particularly of two situations, first, the "gaps" between techniques; and second, finishing techniques. One needs a safe base both to return to and from which to launch attacks. For want of a better word, I usually call this "battery position," following Cassidy in his book, *The Complete Book of Knife Fighting*. As in the case of (hopefully) finishing techniques, this relates to the question of *zanshin* (vigilance upon completion of a technique). It is difficult, and perhaps not necessary, to separate the psychological from the physical form here.

To some extent, long experience and hard practice will usually sort out these transitional gaps, and *kuzushi* (breakdown and analysis of *kata*) and/or *randori* (freestyle sparring), correctly practiced, can be of great assistance here. The danger in the typical martial art is, in the absence of regular experience of actual combat, with its concomitant feedback, that a system that has become too rigid may unwittingly perpetuate misunderstandings of technique.

---

[5] Personal communication, Ellis Amdur.

[6] Whether one is armed or unarmed, and if armed, no matter what weapon one is wielding, the mindset is the same. Personal communication, Hunter B. Armstrong.

A system is faced with the necessity of operating on a number of different levels simultaneously. First, on a purely physical level, the system has to provide a repertoire of practical and effective techniques for its exponents. Second, it has to provide some kind of psychological and behavioral framework. While it is relatively easy for us to observe actual physical technique, it is often very difficult to examine psychological attitudes and behavior. Emic participants are often unconscious of certain behavioral patterns, since to them these are a "given," while etic observers may fail to distinguish clearly between vitally important and irrelevant matters — the "throw the baby out with the bathwater" syndrome. However, we can say that professional warriors have a tendency to develop a pseudo-predatory mindset, i.e. to see other humans as prey, which may serve as a distancing mechanism, giving them a certain immunity against the stress of combat.[7] A key factor here is excitement/arousal. Research indicates increased heart rate is associated with a temporary narrowing of vision, loss of hearing, and loss of fine motor control.[8] While it needs to account for the fact that the exponent may be subject to factors limiting his combative ability, an effective system must also have a program of behavioral conditioning that ideally will enable the exponent to perform at an optimal level despite them.

Thus, what we have to consider in assessing a system's combative viability is not what a highly trained exponent can on occasion make work, but what a reasonably competent student can successfully repeat under less than ideal conditions. A combatively effective system does not need hundreds of techniques. What it needs, or rather demands, are a few tried and proven techniques that work consistently well in a wide range of conditions, both external and internal. By external, I

[7] See Armstrong (1994, 7 no. 2:17), Eibl-Eisenfedt, and Erikson.

[8] "...For example, at 115 beats per minute (BPM) fine motor skills (precision and accuracy skills) deteriorate. When the heart rate exceeds 145 BPM, complex motor skills deteriorate and the visual system begins to narrow. But when the heart rate exceeds 175 BPM, a warrior can expect to experience auditory exclusion, and the loss of peripheral vision and depth perception" (Siddle 1995, 7).

mean those factors such as terrain, visibility, weather, and opponent, which are largely beyond one's control; by internal, those originating in the exponent himself, such as limited combat capacity due to fatigue, hunger, injury, or sickness. When we wish to assess a technique's combative viability, we need to envisage a man whose strength is sapped by diarrhea, wits dulled by lack of sleep over a prolonged period, vision impaired by sweat/rain/dust, slipping in the mud, his fine motor skills falling apart from the stress occasioned by combat. I remember a discussion on precisely this point with Donn Draeger, Hunter Armstrong, and Meik Skoss during the 1979 International Hoplology Society field trip to Malaysia and Indonesia. One of Draeger's suggestions for assessing a technique's combative viability was to do a series of wind sprints, preferably uphill, until one's hands were shaking and one's knees trembling, and then try to make the technique work against a fresh opponent.

I am often surprised by the lack of appreciation of the role played by various limiting factors that sometimes seem to conspire to subvert the best thought-out training programs. Many of us have never been in an army, and even fewer have seen any form of combat (let me hasten to add that I have served in an army, but never saw action), leading to a lack of appreciation of Murphy's Law and the snafu factor. We tend to train for relatively long periods of time under ideal conditions, unaffected by the seasons, weather, or natural or man-made disasters.

A colleague of mine, Tom Dreitlein, wrote these observations about his own training in adverse terrain and weather after reviewing a draft of this piece:

> I trained in smooth-floored indoor dojo for sixteen years in Tokyo and seven years before that in the US. When I moved to Koyasan, I no longer had any access to such facilities. I started training in the hills behind my house.
>
> Meik visited the lower slopes when he was here, and can tell you that they are quite steep. The forest is the standard *sugi* (cedar) forest, and there is a carpet of fallen needles 10 cm or more deep. There are of course any number of roots,

creepers, stones, etc. both visible underfoot and hidden under the forest carpet. I am using the higher slopes for training, which are a bit steeper and rougher.

I have been reexamining what I learned in light of this terrain. Of the many techniques of my ryu, I find that the armor techniques, which constitute an older layer of the ryu, are the ones I can most consistently keep my balance with and execute on this terrain. This is, of course, just the movements done by themselves, and as I have no training partners here, I cannot make comments based on experience regarding paired practice.

I also practice in the snow and on rainy days, and have gotten a number of insights about training under those circumstances. Sub-zero temperatures, 30 cm of snow and a 30 degree or more slope, or deep, slippery mud at twilight are hard taskmasters.

The vast majority of techniques become basically useless, or downright dangerous to the practitioner in this terrain. These techniques are historically documented as being the elaborations of the middle and late Edo period, and this fact concurs with your thesis. Only a shorter spear — no more than seven feet — would be usable. Any techniques with upright erect postures are asking for trouble, especially those that require holding the sword over the head (*jodan kamae*). And I haven't even begun to take wearing armor into consideration.

The area around Koyasan was defended by *sohei* (warrior monks) until the time of Toyotomi Hideyoshi. Hideyoshi brought his forces to the foot of Koyasan, and his assault on Koyasan itself was averted through last-minute diplomacy, but it could easily have ended in the same defeat for the sohei as was experienced at Hieizan during Oda Nobunaga's campaign.

However, the sohei here were obviously trained to conduct defensive operations on the exact same ground that I am practicing on, along some of the old approaches to Koyasan. The content of their training, though still apparently unknown, must have taken these local terrain and weather factors into consideration. In my own inept way I am attempting to recreate something of the parameters of what their training may have involved.

Also, Hideyoshi's forces were undoubtedly prepared for attack on both heavily defended mountain positions and against sohei guerrilla units as at Hieizan.

I am in complete agreement with your K.I.S.S. concept, as there is no other way to look at campaigning in this type of terrain.

It is only in the last hundred years or so that the majority of the population, even in the so-called First World, has become relatively independent of weather and the seasons. Most of us who consider ourselves serious budoka have trained mainly in dojo (thus to some extent independent of the weather and seasons, though air conditioning and heat are by no means universal), and many are proud of their loyalty and consistency in training many years at the same dojo under the same teacher. These are admirable qualities, which I would be the last to disparage; the question I wish to pose is merely, "Was this the norm?"

Personally, I think not. Many of us have spent far more time as students than most of the famous figures we admire. Perilous times; bad communications; the sheer difficulty of traveling over rough country; being away on campaign for months at a time; sickness; wounds and other injuries, either to oneself or others; work and duty, all must have interrupted a warrior's training. In Matsui Kenji's history of the Shinto Muso-ryu, he writes of one teacher, Hirano Kichizo Yoshinobu, (d. 1871) who acted as a courier between his native Fukuoka and Edo, making the strenuous and time-consuming trip with great regularity. Yoshinobu was "said to have made that trip more than one hundred times. At that time, law and order was shaky, road maintenance was haphazard, and vehicles were not used" (14). He was a senior Muso-ryu instructor at the time, but my point is that his masters/employers had their own priorities, which went beyond simply having him instruct others in the ryu. I think anyone who was able to train consistently, i.e. several times a week for more than a few months at a time during a time of war, such as the Sengoku period (1467-1568), would be the exception rather than the rule.

One major exception would probably be those born into the *buke* (warrior houses), who would have unconsciously absorbed much of martial value while growing up in that environment. Otake Risuke Sensei, shihan of the Katori Shinto-ryu, is on record as saying that he has never formally taught his sons Katori Shinto-ryu. In all probability, children would have had a greater opportunity to train consistently over a period of time in the same ryu. Moreover, depending on the domain, children of upper class *bushi* may have been required to attend a *hanko* (domain school), where they would study, among other things, the authorized *ryuha* of that domain (*otome ryu*).

I have recently had a number of discussions with Kato Hiroshi, designated 22nd headmaster of Tatsumi-ryu, on the subject of how children should be trained. We both have 11-year-old sons, so we share a certain amount of interest in the subject. According to him, the advice that has been passed down within the ryu is that the child's natural, relaxed movement is something to be treasured and preserved at all costs. On no account should the child be forced into unnatural movement patterns, or use a sword that is too heavy, as this will lead to bad habits in the future. Better a *bokuto* that is a little too light than one that is too heavy. I was told that the disadvantage of starting iai training too early was that a sword that is too heavy for the user can lead to stiff, forced technique and loss of the ability to relax the hands and arms properly, slowing down techniques. Both he and I have chosen to start our sons with basic kenjutsu techniques, rather than iai. His son is also being sent to kendo dojo, and mine to a judo dojo.

According to Kato Hiroshi Sensei, most people neglected to practice the most basic techniques sufficiently. To him, this is what distinguishes the professional approach from that of the amateur. The professional is prepared to spend a long time working on and polishing the most basic techniques, ad nauseum. Each technique must be worked to

SWORD & SPIRIT

Headmaster designate, Kato Hiroshi, demonstrating kenjutsu with his son, Atsushi, at Shimogamo Shrine, May 1997

perfection. He argues that, leaving aside for a moment the behavioral/psychological components inherent in kata, unless sufficient work has been done on the individual movements that make up that kata, the kata itself loses its meaning. In other words, it is a case of "garbage in, garbage out."

On the whole, I think people have an exaggerated notion of the time the bushi had available for self-training. For the great majority, work and duties probably absorbed most of their time. As children of a modern technological culture, it is hard for us to appreciate what it was like to live during the days of the bushi. You would probably have to live for a while in a village without electricity and motor transport to really understand this.

I live in Chiba Prefecture on Tokyo Bay, and I can drive across to the Pacific side of the peninsula in about an hour. As I drive along the highway that goes through the hills, I sometimes reflect on the effort that such a journey would have involved in the past. The dense

The Tojutsu of the Tatsumi-ryu

woodland and scrub that cover the hills would have made traveling painfully slow and difficult. I don't think it would have helped to go by horse, and I estimate that one would be lucky to do the journey in two days in the past, and that one would have had to be pretty motivated to do so.[9] This is not a particularly dramatic example, but it clearly demonstrates the difficulties involved in doing things that nowadays we tend to take for granted.

Goshi (farmer warriors), who always comprised only a small fraction of the bushi class, must have been very much at the mercy of the weather and seasons, as anybody who knows much about peasant societies will readily appreciate. Come harvest time, the crop must be brought in. It's a simple matter of survival. Again, most of us are far removed from this sort of agricultural society, but those who, like my wife, were brought up on a farm, will understand the point I am trying to make. She can remember all the children being let off school, and the whole village working until late at night to bring in the harvest, the children gradually dropping out as it got late, falling asleep wherever they were. There were things that took priority over training.

Finally, for the *ashigaru* (foot soldiers), many of the same caveats that apply to any conscript force would probably be valid. Over the centuries, combat instructors have been faced with the problem of assembling, equipping, and training large bodies of men, of varying degrees of motivation, in the shortest time possible. Clearly, what needs to be taught are a few, simple techniques that work rather than dozens or even hundreds of techniques.

The Development of Iai

Now, how does all this relate to evaluating the combat effectiveness of training in solo sword drawing techniques? Many people have been exposed to iai through the Zen Nihon Kendo Renmei iai *seiteigata*,

---

[9] A few years ago, an acquaintance of mine decided to try to live off the land in this area for a week, and gave up after a couple of days. He was unable to find enough food to subsist upon, and couldn't stand the leeches.

which stem primarily from the Muso Shinden-ryu and related lines that trace their descent from Hayashizaki Jinsuke Shigenobu (ca. 1542-1621). The spread of this "standardized" form has resulted in a somewhat narrowed idea of the nature of iai and its role as part of an integrated combat training system, such as are found in the *sogo bujutsu*, comprehensive schools that predate the Tokugawa shogunate.

As pointed out in Gordon Warner's and Draeger's *Japanese Swordsmanship*, several styles of iai predate Hayashizaki Jinsuke's formulation. The Tenshin Shoden Katori Shinto-ryu is generally considered the earliest, preceding Hayashizaki Jinsuke's birth by almost one hundred years, and is thought to have had a kind of seed effect, giving rise to or influencing a great number of ryuha. However, as Warner and Draeger state, "swordsmen of the Tatsumi Ryu and the Takenouchi Ryu, both of which traditions were founded in the early half of the sixteenth century and ante-date the birth of Jinsuke, also practiced iai-jutsu, and these two systems are extant today" (80). It is worth noting that these two traditions are almost certainly quite distinct from and independent of the influence of the Katori Shinto-ryu. They are from areas quite remote from the Katori area of what was then known as Shimosa Province (now northern Chiba Prefecture) that gave birth to the Katori Shinto-ryu.

Takenouchi-ryu has always been based in the Okayama area. According to Watatani, the unique form of grappling involving the use of short weapons, known as *kogusoku* or *koshi no mawari*, characteristic of that ryu, is probably a product of specific local conditions (32-33). There is also no technical similarity between Takenouchi-ryu and Katori Shinto-ryu. Thus, given poor communications and the sheer difficulty of traveling through a rugged country at war, this style was almost certainly an independent development.

Tatsumi-ryu is said to have originated in Shikoku. The style became linked to a branch of the Hotta family in what is today Yamagata Prefecture, and followed the clan when the Hotta lord was transferred to the fief centered in Sakura, which is in Shimosa (Papinot 187). Although Tatsumi-ryu was then located fairly near Katori, I am not aware of any kind of influence either way, and the styles themselves are quite distinct in appearance.

While little is known of Tatsumi-ryu founder Tatsumi Sankyo, we do know that he lived during a turbulent period, and that he was a contemporary of the warlord Mori Motonari (1497-1571). He would have found it difficult not to have been drawn into the almost continuous warfare of the period, if not in that particular area, then elsewhere in Japan. According to the Tatsumi-ryu's written traditions, Tatsumi Sankyo trained assiduously in the martial arts from an early age. As a result, he was never defeated, either on the battlefield or in single combat. Finding himself dissatisfied with mere technical proficiency, or even victory in combat, he dedicated himself to the deity Tsumayama Daimyojin to go beyond the superficial levels of purely physical achievement. After arduous training, he attained what in Zen terms is known as *satori*, that is, enlightenment arrived at in an intuitive flash of understanding. He then formulated the Tatsumi-ryu as a result of his experiences in the light of his new understanding.

Similar stories are told of the inspiration leading to the founding of other ryuha. Usually such stories are simply glossed over, but I would like to examine more closely some of the implications inherent in them. A term that often occurs is *kanarazu katsu* (certain victory). At first, this term may seem to be boastful or unrealistic, for we are all aware of the role of chance in battle. However, I believe the true meaning is that the flash of inspiration, the "divine spark," that figures in all these stories is a realization of certain essential physical and related psychological principles underlying victory in combat. All the warriors who founded such systems were men with extensive practical experience in mortal combat, who as a result were able to come to an understanding of what was truly important in combat, and what was not. I believe that the "core" techniques of such systems that have stood the test of time and survive today are the physical manifestation of those principles. It is important to realize that these ryu were not founded in a vacuum, that both the men who founded the ryu and many of those who became their students were fully conversant with a wide range of weapons and techniques. Therefore, I see the ryu as a systemization and ordering, selecting and prioritizing, if you will, of the many and varied fighting/combative techniques such men undoubtedly knew. Draeger argued in one of his lectures that the importance of training could not be overemphasized, and I believe this is an excellent example.

> Training, properly done, reorganizes experience, completely readjusts perceptions, and re-enforces attention to what one is doing. These are the conditions essential, I think, to the fighting man, the one we are dealing with in hoplology. (unpublished audio tape, courtesy Pat Lineberger)

Most Westerners have had only a limited exposure to the wide variety of iai, and the Tatsumi-ryu contains a number of elements that are quite different from what one typically sees. One of the most significant of these differences is the image of the swordsman seated in *seiza*. Draeger points out a number of technical characteristics of the Muso Shinden-ryu that in his opinion indicate a move away from combative effectiveness; the seiza posture, the way the sword is worn, and the curious fact that the kodachi is not used (89). These points apply equally to related styles and modern standardized iai. Most modern Japanese historians believe that seiza was confined to women and priests in the Sengoku period. The year-long historical dramas shown on NHK TV are always careful to show men of that era sitting in the cross-legged *agura* position. The occasional exception is a character such as Sen no Rikyu, founder of the Japanese tea ceremony, and the tea ceremony may indeed have played a role in the spread of seiza among men of the upper classes after the establishment of the Tokugawa shogunate. Farmers, who comprised the majority of the population, would rarely if ever have had either the inclination or the occasion to sit in seiza, and I base this opinion not only on an overview of current historical research, but on numerous visits to a small farming community in Niigata over the past twenty-four years.

I suspect that the establishment of the centralized Ministry of Education in the Meiji era did much to spread the use of seiza throughout

Japan, and to make it common in areas in which it had once been rare. In my experience, men in the country don't usually sit in seiza, indoors or out, and the lovely tatami mats that everyone has nowadays were confined to the upper classes until comparatively recently. Thin straw mats laid on hard wooden floors were much more typical, and did not encourage anyone to sit in seiza for very long, even if they wanted to. When I first visited the three-hundred-year-old farmhouse in Niigata where my wife was born, there were no tatami mats in the living room at all. Country kitchens in the more remote areas were *doma*, earth-floored, again until quite recently, and were often contiguous with stabling for an ox or two, or perhaps a horse, depending on the area. You would not want to sit seiza on that kind of floor, and people didn't.

Tatsumi-ryu iai

Let's begin with a look at the most basic level of technique, the *tachiai*.

While Tatsumi-ryu does make use of the seiza position, it is done only as a variation, not as the basic way of practice. I believe that a unique feature of the ryu is that it emphasizes drawing the sword and cutting while walking in a natural manner. By natural, I mean the way one would walk barefoot, or with only light protection, such as that afforded by *waraji* (straw sandals). Urban dwellers, their feet protected by good shoes, often walk carelessly and inefficiently. Walking barefoot, one tends to take smaller steps in contrast to the strides one is able to take in sturdy shoes. The emphasis is on being able to move easily in any direction (personal communication, Hunter B. Armstrong).

The basic kamae

The most basic kamae is *shizentai*, that is, the natural standing position. One simply stands with one's sword sheathed, with one's hands hanging relaxed at one's sides. One's feet are somewhat closer than they would be in, say, a judo shizentai, because the requirements of swordsmanship differ from those of grappling. One should be perfectly centered when in this position, and should be ready to start walking

Tatsumi-ryu method of holding the sheathed sword

without first displacing body weight to one side or another. The next step is to walk in a natural, perfectly balanced way. A key factor is that one should always be ready to move in any direction with the utmost economy of movement. As soon as one begins to move, the left hand is placed lightly on the *saya* (sheath), immediately behind the *tsuba* (swordguard), with the left index finger resting lightly on the swordguard. In other ryuha, the thumb, or the thumb and index finger, are placed on the guard, and the thumb is used to push on the tsuba to help start the draw. The Tatsumi-ryu prefers not to use the thumb to start the draw, as it is felt that this grip tends to make the left hand tense, and so the wrist is not free to move, and control of the saya becomes more difficult. In Tatsumi-ryu, the idea is for the left hand to control the sheath, *not* the swordguard.

The draw

Both hands work in unison, the left hand turning the sheath, bringing it close to the front of one's body so that the blade of the sword

The Tojutsu of the Tatsumi-ryu

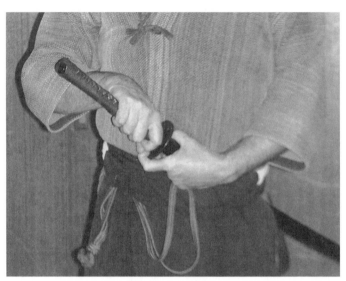

Tatsumi-ryu draw

faces diagonally down toward the ground, while the right hand moves gently across the front of the body to take control of the *tsuka* (swordhilt). It is felt that this position is the best way to start the draw because it gives the swordsman the option of attacking from a number of angles without "signaling" his intentions. Both hands are kept as close to one's body as possible. This minimizes the target available to the opponent, and pulling the hands in toward the body actually provides an additional fraction of distance from one's opponent, an important factor when life or death is a matter of inches. The *kuden* (oral teaching) is that one should feel as if one is drawing the sword with one's stomach, not with one's hands.

There has been a good deal of speculation about how this draw originated. In the past, the swordguard was often tied to the *kurigata* (cord retaining knob) with string, and it would require a firm tug to break the sword free in the draw. A further factor may well have been the sword's size and weight. Analysis of the most central, and thus presumably oldest techniques of the style, along with examination of swords that have been passed down within the ryu, lead me to conclude that we are dealing with movements designed to optimize the use of a weapon that is heavier and longer than the standard sword used in modern iai. The fact that the ryu originated in the Sengoku period when one would be facing opponents wearing armor may possibly account for the preference for a longer, heavier blade, and it has become something of an axiom among hoplologists that the morphology of the weapon dictates technique. I believe that the swords worn with civilian dress would naturally tend to be lighter, for the simple reason that one would not be expecting to meet a fully armored opponent.

Yet a further theory, and in the absence of evidence I must admit this is really pure speculation, is that the Tatsumi-ryu draw is a result of the carry-over of motor patterns acquired in drawing a *tachi*, the kind of sword that was worn with armor, slung from one's belt rather than thrust through a sash. This necessitated that the sheath be grasped firmly, and might also account for the cutting edge being angled down at the beginning of the draw. Alternatively, this may be a case of deliberately designed integration of technique so that it did not matter whether the exponent was wearing a tachi or a *katana*; the basic draw would be done in the same way.

Two central techniques: muko and marui

Two techniques, muko and marui, are at the heart of Tatsumi-ryu. In muko, one's opponent attacks first, and the actual kata involves drawing one's sword, blocking the attack, and delivering a powerful counterstroke before the opponent can recover. This would be classified as *go no sen*. Marui may be thought of as a preemptive attack, and covers the possibilities inherent in *sen no sen* and *sensen no sen*.[10] It begins with a vertical downward cut to the opponents' sword arm; and then, like muko, it follows up immediately with a powerful double-handed cut downward. Not only do these two techniques form the

---

[10] Go no sen is reactive initiative; sen no sen is simultaneous initiative; sensen no sen is preemptive or proactive initiative.

whole basis of Tatsumi-ryu iai, they are also the two most basic kenjutsu techniques. The point of view inherent in this is that there are no *gokui* (inner teachings) in Tatsumi-ryu, or perhaps rather that the basics are the gokui. There is no mystery: the student is at once introduced to the techniques that he will actually use in combat.

There are several key points here: first, all cuts are delivered with the intention of killing or at the very least, severely incapacitating the opponent to the point where he is no longer a serious threat. This relates to my second point, that the movements themselves are biomechanically extremely strong movements, designed to deliver maximum power on impact. Research indicates that although fine and complex motor skill diminishes with increased stress, gross motor skills, involving major muscle groups, are not affected, or performance is actually enhanced under stress.[11]

These two kata, muko and marui, together with six variations, form the first set of eight kata from which all further variations of Tatsumi-ryu iai are derived. The eight techniques comprising the *omote* iaijutsu are: muko; marui; *go no muko* (muko done to the rear); *go no marui* (marui done to the rear); *zengo* (variation on marui involving a 180 degree turn); *hidari* (muko done to the left); *migi* (marui done to the right); *shiho* (variation on marui covering four directions).

This basic set of eight can be done at three levels (jo, ha, kyu), and can be practiced starting either from a standing position (tachiai) or sitting in seiza. As mentioned before, it is the tachiai that is considered to be standard and of far more importance. I personally believe that the sitting techniques, known as *igumi*, were a later development, and probably only came into use after practice was done indoors on a regular basis, but I must admit I have no documentary evidence for my opinion. On the other hand, there is clearly no specific mention of iai done from a sitting position in the early *makimono* (scrolls), and personally I find it difficult to do the techniques in exactly the same way as when standing. To give just one example, the position of the sword as

[11] See Siddle (1998).

SWORD & SPIRIT

Muko, comparing the block in the iai version with the same move in kenjutsu

Below, left, kiri age in muko no kage; right, side view of horizontal cut in marui no kage

The Tojutsu of the Tatsumi-ryu

it is worn in Tatsumi-ryu means that the butt end of the saya is pressed against the floor, and this in turn interferes with the proper execution of the draw.

The jo, ha, kyu division

This division is sometimes compared to a similar system of classification in *shodo* (traditional calligraphy done with a brush), in which the three stages are *kaisho*, *gyosho*, and *sosho*. At the kaisho stage, the character is written in a very plain, basic way. Then, at the gyosho stage, the brush is used in a more natural, flowing manner. Finally, at the sosho stage, shortcuts are taken leading to what may be seen as an abstract and sometimes quite individualistic representation of the character, far removed from the basic kaisho. This system is used not only for the iai techniques, but also for the kenjutsu.

Jo

The basic level of Tatsumi-ryu iai is jo. At this level, beginners work slowly and carefully to learn the correct technique and to familiarize themselves with the use of the sword. Working slowly and carefully provides a kind of safety net, and also enables instructors to monitor the students' progress and make sure that bad habits are avoided, or nipped in the bud. The trainee walks slowly and stops to draw slowly and carefully.

However, it should be noted that slow does not mean that the movements are all executed at the same speed. A theme that runs through the Tatsumi-ryu teachings is that of *in/yo*, possibly more familiar to readers as the Chinese concept of *yin* and *yang*. One of the *densho*, the "Hendo no maki," is primarily concerned with the interplay between hard and soft/flexible, and how a sophisticated understanding of the relationship can enable students of the ryu to work toward increasing the speed and power of their technique. It should be emphasized that this is a very practical concern, and not a merely theoretical or philosophical one. Even when working relatively slowly, the Tatsumi-ryu exponent is expected to demonstrate his practical understanding of this relationship. Thus the experienced observer will note that the draw and cuts are started relatively slowly but the speed increases as the movement proceeds. When performed by an experienced swordsman, this accelerating cut is extremely difficult to avoid or evade.

Ha

This is the intermediate level, and has three levels of *kage* (hidden) techniques associated with it. The trainee learns to use the sword at speed, walks at a normal pace, and the sword is drawn while walking. However, certain movements may seem to be exaggerated, primarily because the student is being taught how to work with the sword, and not against it, very important when using a long, heavy weapon. Although I am describing these levels as basic, intermediate, and advanced, this is somewhat misleading, as once the cycle has been completed, all three levels are used in practice by the advanced exponent. It is felt that each level enables one to work on a different aspect of his technique. Because of the exponent's increasingly effective skills, this cycle will inevitably take on some of the qualities of a spiral, and advanced exponents will be doing the same movements as beginners, but at increasing levels of efficiency and effectiveness.

"Ryu" in kaisho, gyosho, and sosho; calligraphy by Hirato Hiroko

The Tojutsu of the Tatsumi-ryu

Kyu

At this level, the solid muko blocking technique of the jo and ha levels is transformed into a sophisticated deflection. The large circular movements of the previous levels are replaced by fast direct cuts from a relatively upright *jodan kamae*, thus decreasing the distance that the sword has to cover to its target. At this level, the *osame* (the return of the sword to its sheath) is done in a different and technically more difficult way.

Kage

All three sets of kage techniques, *shoden*, *honden*, and *betsuden*, are considered to be variations on the ha level iai. However, within that level, they follow the jo, ha, kyu pattern of doing the same techniques in an increasingly sophisticated way (though the timing does not change and the *noto*, or sheathing of the sword, is always done in ha style). At the kage level, muko begins with an attack instead of a block. The movement of drawing the sword continues smoothly into *kiri age* (a upward diagonal cut), which has as its primary target the underside of one's opponent's right arm as he begins to draw his sword. As in the omote kata, this is followed by a powerful double-handed cut downwards. Marui begins with a horizontal cut to one's opponent's upper arm at the lower point of the deltoid muscle (see photos page 131) . Again, this is followed immediately with a powerful double-handed cut downward. The pattern is obvious, to take care of the immediate threat by disabling the opponent, and then follow up with a killing blow.

Kage introduces the *kesa* (downward diagonal cut), as well as the kiri age already mentioned. Again, these techniques can be practiced either from a standing position (tachiai) or from seiza, in which case they are known as igumi. As usual, the tachiai is emphasized far more than the igumi.

Other iai techniques

Although the omote and kage make up the major portion of the iaijutsu syllabus, there are two other groups of iai techniques. The first is composed of techniques that are traditionally done *zengo sayu*, i.e. to the front, rear, left, and right. Examples of this group are the techniques *ni no tachi*, *zansetsu*, *gassha* and their variations. A further approach is to work on "case studies" of special situations. For example, the makimono explain how to deal with certain situations, such as how to draw your sword when you are suddenly pushed up against a wall. In the teaching *otoshi zashi nukiyo no koto*, the student is advised on how to draw his sword when the sword is wedged upright, almost vertical in the obi. Advanced students will sometimes recreate these situations and practice various responses, but these techniques are not considered to be true kata. The Tatsumi-ryu has always tried to keep the number of core kata relatively small, as it is firmly believed that the mastery of a few key movements is infinitely preferable to spreading oneself too thinly in an attempt to find a response to every hypothetical situation.

Kenjutsu

This insistence on a relatively small number of techniques applicable in a wide variety of situations is clearly demonstrated in the kenjutsu syllabus as well. Tatsumi-ryu kenjutsu has only three core sets of techniques, the omote, the kage (which deals with how to use the short sword), and the *gogo*. As with the iai syllabus, the omote kenjutsu may be practiced at the jo, ha, or kyu level. The six omote kenjutsu techniques are: muko, marui, *maeja*, *hari*, *makiotoshi*, and *taisha*.

The omote techniques pit long sword (tachi) against long sword. This level is primarily concerned with responding to an opponent's attack. The general pattern is to disrupt the attack and immediately counter. The techniques can be done with either *fukuro shinai* (mock swords covered by leather or cloth) or *bokken* (wooden swords). An interesting point is that, in Tatsumi-ryu, only the senior student, who plays the part of the "enemy," uses a jodan kamae.

At the jo level, movement is accompanied by breath control exercises in the form of a vocalized hum, making the student tense his stomach slightly, and having the effect of centering the student. The fukuro shinai is generally used at this level, making it safer for beginners.

Strong technique is developed through repetition of the basic movements. It is common to repeat a block several times in succession to give the maximum amount of practice to the student. Again, walking in a natural manner is emphasized, just as it is in the iai techniques.

I'd like to make a couple of points about this emphasis on walking. It seems to me that something extremely interesting is taking place here. First, there is the contribution that walking must have in terms of mind/body control, for want of a better term. I see walking as an attempt to build a cool, calm attitude to what is actually a very scary thing: mortal combat. This is why I wish to make the distinction between iai coordinated with walking as opposed to striding or moving in a manner calculated to set one's pulse racing. We know now that an increased pulse rate activates the sympathetic nervous system resulting in diminished performance in some areas (Siddle 1995, 1998).

I believe that we first have a deliberate attempt to link a cool mindset or *fudoshin* with iai through the medium of walking, and that further there is a deliberate attempt to transfer this effect to the kenjutsu through the same medium. I believe that the development of this mindset is also encouraged by the practice of teaching the student to block or otherwise defend while walking forward at the jo level. There is a further physiological effect that I am also convinced is planned, albeit it was probably first discovered empirically. Yamada Ichiro, a senior instructor of the ryu, told me that he had noticed that students who had learned the jo form first made far more rapid progress in mastering the two techniques that are concerned with controlling the opponent's sword (hari and makiotoshi). After some discussion, we concluded that walking forward put the students in a situation where they were naturally and unconsciously using the hip action involved in walking together with the action of their hands to do the movement properly. There appears to be a carry-over in that the students who had learned how to do the technique this way, which at first sight does not appear combatively effective, were able to pick up the "real" technique more easily.

Ha

The same techniques are done at the ha level while shifting back slightly, just out of range, providing a margin of safety. The bokken is generally used at this level at present; in the past, however, the fukuro shinai was more commonly used. Once one has achieved a measure of competence at the jo level, this set receives the most emphasis. Techniques are done at normal speed, rather than in the slow, deliberate fashion of the jo set. As is the case with the omote iai set, there is a run-up featured in one technique, in this case, hari. It is arguable that this is a kind of introduction to the kyu set.

Kyu

The kyu level is almost exactly the same as the ha level, but all the kata begin with the two trainees running toward each other. This is a carefully controlled run with short steps as if on a very slippery surface, not an all-out sprint. A number of ryuha I have observed over the years appear to share this idea. The key point is that one should not be so focused on moving forward that one cannot easily change direction. Muko is done in a slightly different way, involving minimum hand movement.

Kage

The kage set teaches the use of the *kodachi* (short sword) against the *odachi* (long sword). The short sword "wins." Kage is mainly concerned with the problem of how to gain entry so as to be able to use the short sword effectively. The three techniques are: *migi irimi* (entry on the right); *hidari irimi* (entry on the left); and *uten saten* (turn right, turn left).

These techniques echo similar movement patterns in other sets, specifically, migi irimi is the same as the last technique in the gogo set; hidari irimi is repeated against the spear in the set of *sojutsu* techniques known as *kodachi awase*; uten saten shows how to apply marui with the short sword to both left and right (see photos on pages 138-139).

*The last technique of gogo no kata (kodachi versus tachi); note
how the movements are the same as those depicted at right,
regardless of the weapon confronted*

SWORD & SPIRIT

A similar technique in kodachi yari awase

The Tojutsu of the Tatsumi-ryu

Gogo

This set consists of five techniques. These techniques represent a distillation of a number of principles of combat and psychological attributes pertaining to combat. The first four techniques are performed with the long sword, and the last with the short sword. In all cases, the opponent is armed with a long sword.

The first technique represents the principle of *taisabaki* (body evasion); one avoids the opponent's attack by moving slightly to the side and simultaneously countering. This is done against both a cut and a thrust. The second technique blends deflection and attack into one movement. The third technique, sometimes called *nioi* (smell or scent), is concerned with anticipating the opponent's attack; to beat him to the punch, as it were. The fourth technique is concerned with psychologically dominating the opponent. One "sets him up," and then takes advantage of his *suki* (opening). It is the first part of this technique that corresponds to the first of the kage set. The fifth technique, the one done with the short sword, is also concerned with dominating the opponent. Superficially, the technique appears to be on the omote level, but in fact the feeling is quite different. The first part of the technique is again a variation on muko as done at the kyu level, but done with a short sword.

The gogo may be practiced in a number of ways, either from a starting position with swords drawn, in which case it looks like the usual kenjutsu kata, or beginning with both sides having their swords sheathed, in which it takes on a different, iai-like flavor.

Fudoshin: the combative mindset

Among the ryu's teachings is an admonition of the various pitfalls to be avoided. Some are enumerated as follows: fear, doubt, anger, hesitation, and surprise. Ideally, one should be a state of *munen muso* (no ideas, no desires, no thoughts). The ideal is to be able to absorb every nuance of the opponent's movements, without in turn providing any feedback. In explaining this to me, Kato Takashi Sensei gave as an example a radio that receives messages, but does not send. I remember Meik Skoss, after watching a senior of mine, Kankei Keiichi, demonstrate the kenjutsu, commenting on precisely this point: that even as a highly experienced emic observer of Japanese kenjutsu, it was hard for him to guess what the swordsman was going to do next. This is one manifestation of "invisibility."[12]

These three sets, omote, kage, and gogo, form the core of the Tatsumi-ryu kenjutsu syllabus. However, since the Tatsumi-ryu's primary weapon is the sword, and the sword "wins" the kata when facing the *bo*, *hanbo*, and *naginata*, it could well be argued that these sets form part of the kenjutsu syllabus too. In any case, they are definitely subsumed within the tojutsu. An important point that I would like to make here is that of parsimony of technique. It is not necessary for the swordsman to learn new ways of using the sword to counter each new weapon. The swordsman learns to defeat these weapons using essentially the same techniques he has acquired in his study of the core kenjutsu kata. Let me give some specific examples.

In the first kata against the bo, the sword uses the second technique of the omote level kenjutsu, marui, to enter and attack. The kata ends with the sword performing the same finishing move as the last omote kenjutsu kata, taisha.

Attacks along the same line, whether the opponent uses a bo, hanbo, or naginata, are treated in the same manner. A diagonal overhead attack to the left side of the head is deflected, and the swordsman cuts *do* to the body (see photos on pages 142-143).

There are four further sets using swords, which, while not central to the kenjutsu syllabus, at the very least deserve to be included under the tojutsu label. These are *niozume* (techniques showing how to use the long and the short swords in conjunction), *seiganzume* (techniques for defeating an opponent armed with two swords), *teto* (techniques for using the sheathed sword), and the *yari awase tachi kachimi* (techniques against the spear where the sword wins).

The Tatsumi-ryu has a reputation for being very *jimi* (plain) as opposed to *hade* (flashy). Its saving grace, I was told by several people

[12] See Hall (100).

*A diagonal overhead attack to the left side of the head is
deflected, and the swordsman cuts the body; naginata awase*

Same pattern of movement with a hanbo; different weapons are defeated in similar ways

The Tojutsu of the Tatsumi-ryu

who seemed knowledgeable in this area, is that it really works. Efficient biomechanical movements, economy of technique, parsimony of technique, and integration of technique serve to make this a severely functional and deadly system.

Iai and Kenjutsu

Now for some general remarks on the relationship between iai and kenjutsu. Iai and kenjutsu work together like the two wheels of a cart. In other words, they are both necessary and they complement each other. A cart with one wheel isn't going anywhere. At best, it is a vehicle fit only for display — flower arranging perhaps?

It is probably useful to remember the distinction between open and closed sports here. Just to remind you, golf is an example of a "closed" sport. When you play golf, you generally don't have to worry about being hit by your opponent's ball, or your opponent trying to hit you over the head when you tee off. Tennis, on the other hand, is an "open" sport, in that one is directly affected by what one's opponent does, and one is forced to respond in one way or another.

While I know we are not talking about sports here, it seems to me that iai and kenjutsu do fit quite neatly into these slots. Hunter Armstrong made a strong case for kenjutsu in his article, "The Koryu Bujutsu Experience." Let me play devil's advocate and see if I can list the advantages for practicing iai. I should emphasize that these remarks pertain to the practice of iai as a complement to kenjutsu, not to iai practiced in isolation. Further, I would urge that much of the value of the complementary practice is lost if the iai and kenjutsu do not form an integrated system. In other words, practicing seiteigata iai to complement your kendo training will not, at least in my opinion, result in a viable system for combat. Training in iai without corresponding kenjutsu practice may lead to what Draeger refers to as "combatively inane" practices.

However, even "open" sports like tennis do make some use of "closed" training. One thinks of tennis players knocking the ball against the wall, karateka hitting the *makiwara*, judoka practicing footsweeps on heavy bags, and so on. Quite obviously, this does not constitute the major portion of their training, but it can be useful to practice techniques in this way on occasion. So possibly the question for the serious student becomes, in what proportions should one practice kenjutsu and iai? This boils down to personal circumstances and interests, and I don't know if there is anything more useful that I can say here, except to remark that the problem is not as simple as one might think, given that we are talking about qualitatively different kinds of practice. The very intensity of proper kenjutsu practice probably precludes spending too much time on it, whereas one could profitably practice iai on a daily basis. The danger here is that the more time one spends on kenjutsu, the more the temptation to make it safer in one way or another comes to the fore. In fact, this accounts for the development of kendo.

The advantages of practicing iai are those of practicing any solo form: first, one can practice at one's own convenience, relatively free from the constraints of having to fit in with others; further, one has the opportunity to work on technique safely and without extraneous distraction, being able to acquire useful transferable skills through repetitive practice. The fact that you are working with a live blade is not to be dismissed lightly. At the very least, you are acquiring competence with the precise weapon you would in fact be using in combat. In my own training, I have found it of value to work solo through portions of the kenjutsu syllabus, after my regular iai practice. I have also found that the extra weight of the *shinken* (live blade) as opposed to the bokuto makes a definite difference to the feel of the techniques.

CONCLUSION

In my opinion, if a classical Japanese ryuha has hundreds of techniques, these are very probably the result of elaboration during long periods of peace, rather than the products of a time of war. When a group is at war, no one has the time either to teach or learn hundreds of techniques. At the risk of being thought sarcastic, if your style has a twenty-year training program, and most people start in their late teens, they are going to be in their late thirties, and past their physical peak, before they are theoretically ready for combat. By this time the war they have been training for is probably over. There is no society that can afford this kind of inefficiency; if there ever was, it was wiped out long ago. The nature of war itself would not permit it to survive. The whole history of warfare is one of struggling to do the best one can against the odds, often at short notice, with inadequately trained troops and insufficient resources. A further factor affecting training is the intensity of the program itself. I will not examine this factor in depth at this time because I think my argument is still valid without it. However, let me just observe that training with the actual prospect of using what one is learning in the very near future is of an order quite different to that of doing a martial art for its possible self-defense value at some vague future date. Dr. Samuel Johnson wrote, "Depend upon it, Sir, when a man knows he is to be hanged in a fortnight, it concentrates his mind wonderfully." Similarly, the prospect of engaging in mortal combat in the immediate future lends an entirely new dimension to training for the more motivated; while for those less well motivated, the de facto power of life and death that any army must have in wartime to be at all effective becomes itself a motivating factor. To look at some modern examples, basic training seems to have averaged out at about six weeks during the First and Second World Wars; nowadays it is eight weeks for the US Army and eleven weeks for the Marines. Perhaps not directly relevant but nevertheless highly instructive, is Robert Graves' estimate of how long it took for an officer to become fully efficient in World War I trench warfare: a mere three weeks.[13] This may be categorized as "on the job" training, but this kind of training — fine tuning to the demands of the immediate combative environment — may have been far more common than one would think and deserves serious consideration.

[13] "Between three weeks and four weeks he [the officer] was at his best, unless he happened to have any particular bad shock or sequence of shocks. Then his usefulness gradually declined... by nine or ten months, unless he had been given a few weeks rest on a technical course, or in a hospital, he usually became a drag on the other company officers" (143).

Reluctant or not, conscripts have to be taught a few simple techniques that will enable them to handle a wide variety of situations in less than ideal conditions. In any case, given the typically limited time at one's disposal, and the workings of Murphy's Law, once again it is only sound common sense to use the so-called k.i.s.s. principle: Keep It Short and Simple. Indeed, there are many examples of training hastily conducted in a matter of hours.[14] While the immediate needs of a particular conflict may call for widely differing responses, the principles of efficiency, economy, parsimony, and integration of technique are absolutes that will transcend the particular situation and provide us a conceptual framework with which to judge a system's combative viability.

Acknowledgements

I am indebted to many friends and colleagues for literally hundreds of stimulating conversations, some beginning over twenty years ago, some more recently: Ellis Amdur, Hunter Armstrong, George Bristol, Tom Dreitlein, David Hall, Steve Kelsey, and Meik and Diane Skoss.

I owe a great debt of gratitude to my teachers, Kato Takashi Sensei and Kato Hiroshi Sensei, for their painstaking teaching, their explanations and elucidations of the many makimono still preserved by the ryu, and their many kindnesses over the past fourteen years; to my senior Yamada Ichiro, a senior instructor of the ryu, for his friendship, good humor, and encouragement of my research; and to my senior Kankei Kenichi, a man of the highest standards, for whom only the best is ever good enough, whose example has inspired me. I thank Yamada Ichiro and another of my seniors, Kashimura Norihisa, for taking time out of their busy schedules to pose for the kenjutsu photographs. The motor drive camera with which the photographs were taken was kindly lent to me by my senior, Fujisaki Yoshinori.

---

[14] See Holmes for a short discussion of this (365).

The Tojutsu of the Tatsumi-ryu

References

Armstrong, H.B. 1994. The Two Faces of Combatives. *Hoplos* 7, no. 2 (part 1) & 3 (part 2).

———. 1997. The Koryu Bujutsu Experience. In *Koryu Bujutsu: Classical Warrior Traditions of Japan,* edited by D. Skoss. Berkeley Heights, NJ: Koryu Books.

Cassidy, W.L. 1975. *The Complete Book of Knife Fighting.* Boulder, Colorado: Paladin Press.

Cooper, J. 1983. Combat Handguns. *International Combat Arms.* Guns and Ammo Series, No. 4.

Draeger, D.F. 1973. *Classical Budo.* The Martial Arts and Ways of Japan, 2. New York & Tokyo: Weatherhill.

Eibl-Eibesfeldt, I. 1979. *The Biology of Peace & War.* New York: The Viking Press.

Erikson, E.H. 1966. Ontogeny of Ritualization in Man. *Philosophical Transactions of the Royal Society.* 251: 337-49.

Graves, R. 1960. *Goodbye to All That.* Penguin Modern Classics.

Hall, D.A. 1997. Marishiten: Buddhist Influences on Combative Behavior. In *Koryu Bujutsu: Classical Warrior Traditions of Japan,* edited by D. Skoss. Berkeley Heights, NJ: Koryu Books.

Holmes, R. 1985. *Acts of War.* New York: The Free Press.

Kaku K. 1987. Mukou. *Kendo Nippon* 12: 100.

———. 1988. Marui. *Kendo Nippon* 1: 88.

Keeley, L. 1988. The Tatsumi-ryu. *Japan Martial Arts Society Newsletter* 6, 2: 2-7.

———. 1997. Kato Takashi: Reflections of the Tatsumi-ryu Headmaster. In *Koryu Bujutsu: Classical Warrior Traditions of Japan,* edited by D. Skoss. Berkeley Heights, NJ: Koryu Books.

Matsui K. 1993. *The History of Shindo Muso Ryu Jojutsu.* Kamuela, Hawaii: International Hoplology Society.

Papinot, E. 1972. *Historical and Geographical Dictionary of Japan.* Rutland, VT & Tokyo, Japan: Charles E. Tuttle Co.

Siddle, B. 1995. *Sharpening the Warrior's Edge.* Millstadt, IL: PPCT Management Systems.

———. 1998. Scientific and Test Data Validating the Isosceles and Single Hand Point Shooting Techniques. *The Firearms Instructor* 25.

Tatsumi-ryu. 1998. *Tatsumi-ryu no Kata.* Sakura: Privately published.

Tatsumi-ryu no Iaijutsu to Sono Kenri. 1992. *Hiden Bujutsu* 9.

Tatsumi-ryu: Sakura Shibu. 1996. *Kendo Jidai* 3: 81-85.

Tatsumi-ryu to Kendo no Setten. 1978. *Kendo Nippon* 5: 7.

Warner, G., and D.F. Draeger. 1982. *Japanese Swordsmanship: Technique and Practice.* New York and Tokyo: Weatherhill.

Watatani K. 1987. The Takenouchi-ryu. *Hoplos* 5, no. 3/4: 32-33.

Yamamoto T. 1988. Bunburyodo no Kuni, Iai mo Okotarazu. *Kendo Jidai* 3: 38-45.

*Karl Friday is a professor of history at the University of Georgia. He is the author of **Hired Swords: The Rise of Private Warrior Power in Early Japan** (1992) and **Legacies of the Sword: The Kashima-Shinryu and Samurai Martial Culture** (1997). He has spent a number of years living, training, and doing research in Japan; he presently holds the menkyo kaiden license and is a certified shihan in Kashima-Shinryu. This article previously appeared in the **Journal of Asian Martial Arts** (1995 4:4), and is reprinted with the kind permission of author and publisher.*

KABALA IN MOTION
KATA & PATTERN PRACTICE IN THE TRADITIONAL BUGEI

Karl F. Friday

The term "*ryuha*," prosaically translated as "school," can be more literally and more evocatively rendered as "branch of the current." The current here represents the onward flow of a stream of thought — an approach to martial art — through time; the branches betoken the partitioning of those teachings, the splitting off that occurs as insights are passed from master to students, generation after generation. Ryuha do not exist to foster skill in combat and the use of weaponry, but to hand on knowledge. For skill cannot be taught or learned, it can only be acquired, through long training and practice — and can be gained nearly as readily without as with a teacher who has himself mastered the art. Skill is, for the most part, self-discovered, imposed on the student from within by his own aptitude and discipline. But knowledge can be bequeathed. The perceptions, inspirations, experiences and wisdom collected over the course of a lifetime by a master of an art can be imparted to students so that each generation can build on the privity of those that came before and each new student will not have to begin the process of discovery from scratch.

The essence of a ryuha, then, can be found in the transmission of its kabala. The essence of that transmission can be found in *kata*, the oldest and still the central methodology for teaching and learning the body of knowledge that constitutes a traditional ryuha.

Few facets of Japanese martial art have been as consistently and ubiquitously misunderstood, even by those who practice them, as kata. Variously described as a kind of ritualized combat; exercises in aesthetic movement; a means to sharpen fundamentals, such as balance and coordination; a type of moving meditation; or a form of training akin to shadow-boxing, kata embraces elements of all these characterizations, but its essence is captured by none of them. Kata, in fact, defies succinct explanation.

The standard English translation for "kata" is "form" or "forms"; but while this is linguistically accurate, the nature and function of kata are better conveyed by the phrase "pattern practice." Fundamentally, kata represents a training method wherein students rehearse combinations of techniques and counter-techniques, or sequences of such combinations, arranged by their teachers. In most cases, students work in pairs.[1] One partner is designated as the attacker or opponent, and is often referred to as *uchidachi* (when he uses a sword), *uchite* (when he uses any other weapon), or *ukete* (when he is unarmed). The other employs the techniques the kata is designed to teach, and is called the *shidachi* (in sword training) or the *shite* (when training unarmed or with other weapons).[2]

This sort of pattern practice provides continuity within the ryuha from generation to generation, even in the absence of written instruments for transmission. The kata practiced by a given ryuha can and do change from generation to generation — or even within the lifetime of an individual teacher — but they are normally considered to have been handed down intact by the founder or some other important figure in the school's heritage. "In order," observed Edo period commentator Fujiwara Yoshinobu, "to transmit the essence of the school [*ryugi no honshitsu*] to later generations, one must teach faithfully, in a manner not in the slightest different from the principles [*jiri*] of the previous teachers."[3] Changes, when they occur, are viewed as being superficial, adjustments to the outward form of the kata; the key elements — the

---

[1] Western audiences usually equate kata training with the solo exercises of Chinese, Okinawan, and Korean martial arts. But pattern practice in the Japanese *bugei* is fundamentally different from this sort of exercise. One important — and obvious — distinction is that kata in both traditional and modern Japanese fighting arts nearly always involve the participation of two or more people.

[2] These terms vary from tradition to tradition.

marrow — of the kata do not change. By definition, more fundamental changes (when they are made intentionally and acknowledged as such) connote the branching off of a new ryuha (cf. Tomiki 42-56, 60).

THE NATURE OF KATA & PATTERN PRACTICE

One of the key points to be understood about pattern practice in the traditional *bugei* is that it serves as the core of training and transmission. In modern Japanese martial arts, such as kendo or judo, kata is often only one of several more or less co-equal training methods, but in the older ryuha, pattern practice was and is the pivotal method. Many schools teach only through pattern practice. Others employ adjunct learning devices, such as sparring, but only to augment kata training, never to supplant it.

The importance of pattern practice comes from the belief that it is the most efficient vehicle for passing knowledge from teacher to student. On one level, a ryuha's kata form a living catalog of its curriculum and a syllabus for instruction. Both the essence and the sum of a ryuha's teachings — the postures, techniques, strategies, and philosophy that comprise a school's kabala — are contained in its kata. And the sequence in which students are taught the kata is usually fixed by tradition and/or by the headmaster of the school. In this way pattern practice is a means to systematize and regularize training. But the real function of kata goes far beyond this.

Mastery of the bugei or other traditional Japanese arts is a supra-rational process. The most important lessons cannot be conveyed by overt explanation, they must be experienced directly; the essence of a ryuha's kabala can never be wholly extrapolated, it must be intuited from examples in which it is put into practice. David Slawson, discussing the art of gardening, describes traditional learning as taking place through an "osmosis-like process, through the senses, with little

<hr>

[3] *Menhyoho no Ki*, quoted in Nakabayashi (1988, 161-62). The date of publication of this text is unkown, but it is believed to have been written in the late Edo period. The ryuha discussed is one from the Shinkage-ryu tradition, transmitted within the Nabeshima family.

theorizing into the underlying principles" (54). His observations echo those of a late Tokugawa period commentator on the bugei:

> Theory [*narai*] is not to be taught lightly; it is to be passed on a little at a time to those who have achieved merit in practice, in order to help them understand the principles [of the art]. Theory, even if not taught, will develop spontaneously with the accumulation of correct training. (Fujiwara, *Menhyoho no Ki*, quoted in Nakabayashi 1988, 165)

The role of the teacher in the bugei tradition then, is to serve as model and guide, not as lecturer or conveyor of information. The standard appellation for teachers of traditional arts, "*shihan*," reflects this role. Although commonly translated as "instructor" or "master instructor," the term literally means something more on the order of "master and model." Bugei teachers lead students along the path to mastery of their arts, they do not tutor them. Issai Chozan's early eighteenth century classic text on swordsmanship, *Neko no Myojutsu*, concludes with an eloquent statement of this principle:

> The teacher only transmits the technique and illuminates its principle. To acquire its truth is within oneself. [In Zen Buddhism] this is called self-attainment; or it may also be called mind-to-mind transmission or special transmission outside the texts. Learning in this fashion does not subvert the doctrines [of the texts], for even a teacher could not transmit [in that way]. Nor is such learning found only in the study of Zen, for in the meditations of the Confucian sages and in all of the arts, mastery lies in mind-to-mind transmission, special transmission outside the texts. Texts and doctrine merely point to what one already has within oneself but cannot see on one's own. Understanding is not bestowed by the teacher. Teaching is easy; listening to doctrines is also easy; but to find with certainty what is within oneself, to make this one's own, is difficult. [In Zen] this is

called seeing one's nature. Enlightenment is an awakening from the dream of delusion; it is the same as understanding. This does not change. (reproduced in Watanabe 15)

To say that understanding comes from within the student should not, however, imply that mastery of the martial (or other) arts mostly involves some mystical discovery of truths preexisting but buried within the self, or some magical bursting forth of the learner's inner being. Quite the contrary, bugei instruction prescribes a gradual, developmental process in which teachers help students to internalize the key precepts of ryuha doctrine. Understanding — mastery — of these precepts comes from within, the result of the student's own efforts. But the teacher presents the precepts, and creates an environment in which the student can absorb and comprehend them, from without.[4] The overall process can be likened to teaching a child to ride a bicycle: the child does not innately know how to balance, pedal and steer, nor will he be likely to discover how on his own. At the same time, no one can fully explain any of these skills either; one can only demonstrate them and help the child practice them until he figures out for himself which muscles are doing what at which times to make the actions possible.

To fully appreciate the function of pattern practice as a teaching and learning device, it is important to understand just what it is that is supposed to be taught and learned, and the relationship of this knowledge to kata. The essential knowledge — the kabala — of a ryuha can be broken down into three components: *hyoho* — or *heiho* — (strategy), *tenouchi* (skill or the application of skill), and *waza* (techniques or tactics). Hyoho refers to something along the lines of "the essential principles of martial art," wherein "essential" is taken in its original meaning of "that which constitutes the essence." As such, hyoho designates the general principles around which a ryuha's approach to combat is

---

[4] G. Victor Sogen Hori discusses at considerable length the notion of Development versus Self-Discovery (his terms), as it applies to Rinzai Zen Buddhist training in "Teaching and Learning in the Rinzai Zen Monastery" (25-32).

constructed: the rationale for choosing between defensive or offensive tactics, the angles of approach to an opponent, the striking angles and distances appropriate to various weapons, the proper mental posture to be employed in combat, the goals to be sought in combat, and similar considerations. Tenouchi constitute the fundamental skills required for the application of hyoho, such as timing, posture, the generation and concentration of power, and the like. Waza are the situationally specific applications of a ryuha's hyoho and tenouchi, the particularized tactics in and through which a student is trained. Waza, tenouchi, and hyoho are functionally inseparable; hyoho is manifested in and by waza through tenouchi.

Kata, then, are compendiums of waza, and as such are manifestations of all three components. More importantly, they are the means by which a student learns and masters first tenouchi and then hyoho. As Fujiwara Yoshinobu observed:

> Technique and principle are indivisible, like a body and its shadow; but one should emphasize the polishing of technique. The reason for this is that principle will manifest itself spontaneously in response to progress in technical training. One should vociferously stifle any impulses to verbally debate principle. (*Menhyoho no Ki*, quoted in Nakabayashi 1988, 166)

In emphasizing ritualized pattern practice and minimizing analytical explanation, bugei masters blend ideas and techniques from the two educational models most familiar to medieval and early modern Japanese warriors, Confucianism and Zen. Kata training first of all shares elements with the Zen traditions of *ishin denshin*, or "mind-to-mind transmission" and what Victor Hori terms "teaching without teaching." The former stresses the importance of a student's own immediate experience over explicit verbal or written explanation, engaging the deeper layers of a student's mind and by-passing the intellect; the latter describes a learning tool applied in Rinzai monasteries whereby students are assigned jobs and tasks that they are expected to learn and

SWORD & SPIRIT

perform expertly with little or no formal explanation. Both force the student to fully invoke his powers of observation, analysis and imagination in order to comprehend where he is being steered. Both lead to a level of understanding beyond cognition of the specific task or lesson presented.[5]

But learning through pattern practice probably derives most directly from Confucian pedagogy and its infatuation with ritual and ritualized action. This infatuation is predicated on the conviction that man fashions the conceptual frameworks he uses to order — and thereby comprehend — the chaos of raw experience through action and practice. One might describe, explain, or even defend one's perspectives by means of analysis and rational argument, but one cannot *acquire* them in this way. Ritual is stylized action, sequentially structured experience that leads those who follow it to wisdom and understanding. Those who seek knowledge and truth, then, must be carefully guided through the right kind of experience, if they are to achieve the right kind of understanding. For the early Confucians, whose principle interest was the proper ordering of the state and society, this meant habitualizing themselves to the codes of what they saw as the perfect political organization, the early Chou dynasty. For bugei students, it means ritualized duplication of the actions of past masters.[6]

In point of fact, Confucian models — particularly the Chu Hsi Neo-Confucian concept of investigating the abstract through the concrete and the general through the particular, but also the Wang Yang Ming (Oyomei) version of Neo-Confucianism's emphasis on the necessity of unifying knowledge and action — dominated all aspects of traditional samurai education, not just the bugei.[7] The central academic subjects of such an education were calligraphy and the reading of the

[5] Hori (11-12). The similarity of bugei training to Zen practices has been noted by a number of observers. See, for example, Suzuki (87-214), or Draeger (63-65).

[6] Robert Eno (6-13, 68-69) offers an insightful and provocative discussion of the meaning of ritual in early Confucianism.

[7] For a general introduction to Neo-Confucianism, see Fung (266-318).

Namiki Yasushi Sensei performing kata of the Heki-ryu
Sekka-ha at Kashima Shrine, ca. 1983.

Confucian classic texts, in Chinese. Calligraphy was taught almost entirely by setting students to copy models provided by their teacher. Students would repeatedly practice brushing out characters that imitated as closely as possible those that appeared in their copy books as the teacher moved from student to student to observe and offer corrections. Reading too, was to be learned through what Ronald Dore describes as "parrot-like repetition" (127). After the teacher slowly read off a short passage — usually no more than four or five characters and at most half a page — from the text, students were directed to recite the

SWORD & SPIRIT

passage over and over again for themselves, until they had mastered its form. Once this was achieved, the teacher would offer some general idea of the meaning of the passage, and the students would return to their practice. Such instruction formed virtually the whole of a young student's first five to seven years of training. The method showed little concern for comprehension of content and offered little or no systematic analysis or explanation of even the principles of Chinese grammar and syntax or of the meanings of individual characters. Rather, it was expected that once acquainted with enough examples, the student would acquire the principles underlying them in gestalt-like fashion. The idea was that learning to recite texts in this fashion was a necessary preparatory step to true reading. Having mastered the former, the student at length moved on to the latter, revisiting the same Confucian classics he had been struggling through for years but now with the goal of comprehending their meaning rather than just their form. Toward this end teachers offered lectures and written commentaries on the texts, but the principal pedagogical tool was still individual practice and repetition, interspaced with regular sessions, in which the teacher would quiz students on difficult passages and incite them to work their way through them (Dore 124-52).

In the light of this, the value medieval and early modern Japanese bugei instructors placed on kata should hardly be surprising. But the notion that "ritual formalism" — in which "students imitate form without necessarily understanding content or rationale" — can lead to deeper understanding and spontaneity of insight than can rational instruction — in which the teacher attempts to articulate the general principles of a task and transmit these to students — is not entirely foreign to Western education either, as Victor Hori observes:

> As a graduate student in philosophy, I taught propositional logic to first- and second-year university students and noticed that the class divided into two groups, those who could solve the logic problems and those who could not. Those who could solve them started by memorizing the basic transformation formulae of propositional logic.... Having

committed these formulae to memory, these students were thereby able to solve the logic problems because they could "just see" common factors in the equations and then cancel them out, or could "just see" logical equivalences. However, the other students, those who had not committed the trans-formation formulae to memory, were more or less mystified by the problems though many made serious attempts to "reason" their way through… those who had done the rote memory work had developed logical insight.[8]

Pattern practice in Japanese bugei also bears some resemblance to medieval Western methods of teaching painting and drawing, in which art students first spent years copying the works of old masters, learning to imitate them perfectly, before venturing on to original works of their own. Through this copying, they learned and absorbed the secrets and principles inherent in the masters' techniques, without consciously ana-lyzing or extrapolating them. In like manner, kata are the "works" of a ryuha's current and past masters, the living embodiment of the school's teachings. Through their practice, a student makes these teachings a part of him and later passes them on to students of his own.

It is important, however, not to lose sight of the fact that kata are a means to mastery of a ryuha's kabala, expressions of that kabala; they are not the kabala itself. Mastery of pattern practice is not the same as mastery of the art: a student's training *begins* with pattern practice, but it is not supposed to end there. Kata are not, for example, intended to be used as a kind of database mechanically applied to specific combat situations ("when the opponent attacks with technique 7-A, respond with counter-technique 7-A.1, unless he is left-handed, in which case…"). Rather, pattern practice is employed as a tool for teaching and learning the principles that underlie the techniques that make up

---

[8] Hori (5-7). Pattern practice and drill are also the key to the highly successful Kumon and Suzuki programs for teaching academic and musical skills in contemporary Japan. "The Kumon Approach to Teaching and Learning" (Ukai 87-113), is an enlightening discussion of the former.

the kata. Once these principles have been absorbed, the tool is to be set aside.

Viewed, then, from the perspective of a student's lifetime, pattern practice is a temporary expedient in his training and development. The eventual goal is for the student to move beyond codified, technical applications to express the essential principles of the art in his own unique fashion, to transcend both the kata and the waza from which they are composed, just as art students moved beyond imitation and copying to produce works of their own.[9]

As he moves toward mastery of the ryuha's teachings, the bugei student's relationship with his school's kata evolves through three stages, expressed by some authorities as "Preserve, Break, and Separate" ("*mamoru, yabureru, hanareru,*" or "*shu ha ri*"). In the first stage he attempts to merge himself into the kata, to bury his individuality within its confines. He is made to imitate the movements and postures of his teachers exactly, and is allowed no departure from the ordained pattern. When he has been molded to the point at which it is difficult for him to move or react in any fashion outside the framework of the kata, he is pushed on to the next stage, wherein he consciously seeks to break down this framework and step outside it. He experiments with variations on the patterns he has been taught, probing their limits and boundaries, and in the process sharpening and perfecting his grasp of the principles that underlie the forms. Only when he has accomplished this can he move on the final stage, the stage of true mastery. Here he regains his individuality. Whereas previously he merged himself *into* the kata, he now emerges fused *with* the kabala of the ryuha. He moves freely, unrestricted by the framework of the kata, but his movements and instincts are wholly in harmony with those of the kata.

---

[9] This concept is emphasized by many bugei ryuha in their choice of orthography for "kata." While most non-martial traditional Japanese arts, such as *chanoyu, shodo,* or *ikebana,* use the character "型," most bugei schools write it with "形," with the explanation that the former implies a rigidity and constraint inappropriate to martial training. The latter, it is argued, better represents the freedom to respond and change — albeit within a pattern — essential to success in combat.

Historical Problems & Criticisms of Kata & Pattern Practice

Pattern practice is a time-honored and, when properly conducted, an efficacious means of training and transmission of knowledge, but it is not without its pitfalls. It is easy to imagine that a methodology centered on imitation and rote memorization could readily degenerate into stagnation and empty formalism. The historical record indicates that this was already becoming a problem for bugei ryuha in Japan by the late seventeenth century.

Certificates of achievement and similar documents left by fifteenth and sixteenth century martial art masters suggest that kata had become the principle means of transmission by this time.[10] It was not, however, the only way in which warriors learned how to fight. Most *bushi* built on insights gleaned from pattern practice with experience in actual combat. This was, after all, the "Age of the Country at War," when participation in battles was both the goal and the motivation for martial training. A number of the most illustrious swordsmen of the age, moreover, including Tsukahara Bokuden, Kamiizumi Ise-no-kami, Miyamoto Musashi, Yagyu Sekishusai Muneyoshi, Yagyu Hyogonosuke, and Ito Kagehisa, are known to have traveled about the country seeking instruction and engaging in duels and sparring matches, a practice, known as *musha shugyo*, which many authorities believe to have been common among serious bugei students. Ordinarily, such students would begin their instruction with a teacher near their home, train with him until they had absorbed all they could, and then set out on the road, offering and accepting challenges from practitioners of other styles. Warriors defeated in such matches (if they survived unmaimed) often became the students of those who bested them.[11]

---

[10] Examples of such documents are reproduced in *Nihon Budo Taikei* (Imamura 1:14, 20-21; 2:402-3, 439-62; 3:12-13) and *Nihon Budo no Engen: Kashima-Shinryu* (Seki 30-32).

[11] Ishioka, Wakada, and Kato (15-18); Nakabayashi (1982, 10: 40-42); Kurogi (159-93). Tominaga asserts that musha shugyo served a double purpose, helping a warrior to

Training conditions altered considerably in the decades after the battle of Sekigahara. First, the new Tokugawa shogunate placed severe restrictions on the freedom of samurai to travel outside their own domains. Second, the teaching of martial arts began to emerge as a profession. Adepts no longer divided their energies between training students and participation in war, as there were no longer wars in which to participate. Instead, they began to open training halls and devote themselves full time to instructing students, who paid fees for their training. And third, contests between practitioners from different schools (*taryu jiai*), became frowned upon by both the government and many of the ryuha themselves.[12]

One result of these developments was a rapid proliferation of new ryuha, spurred at least in part by the disappearing need for "masters" to prove their skills in public combat.[13] A second was a tendency for ryuha, their kabala no longer subject to continual polishing and

---

both hone his martial skills and attract the attention and interest of potential employers (50-51, 63-69). Accounts of specific musha shugyo adventures can be found in *Kengo no Meishobu 100 Wa* (Inagaki 1982), *Nihon Kengodan* (Kobe 1984), *Kengo Shidan* (Okada 1984), *Nihon Kengo 100 Sen* (Watatani 1971), and *Lives of Master Swordsmen* (Sugawara 1985).

[12] The conventional wisdom among the Japanese authorities on this topic attributes the decline of taryu jiai and musha shugyo to prohibition edicts issued in the mid seventeenth century by the shogunate and quickly echoed by the lords of numerous domains and by many of the ryuha themselves; see, for example, Ishioka, Wakada, and Kato (20), Nakabayashi (1982, 10:72-74) or Tominaga (272-75). A word of caution on this point is in order, however: the bans on taryu jiai are mentioned by most studies of the subject, but I have been unable to identify the specific dates for the bans or to locate a primary source confirming them. Moreover, neither taryu jiai nor musha shugyo disappeared completely, as the numerous accounts of celebrated duels during the middle and late Tokugawa period attest. In fact, Tominaga (273) quotes two documents from the late seventeenth century, one issued by the government of the Tsuyama domain in Mimasaka province and the other by a bugei school (the Asayama Ichiden-ryu), that both imply a general prohibition on taryu jiai to have existed but also outline circumstances under which such contests were to be permitted. This is further evidence that duels and matches were still occurring, even if with restrictions.

refinement through exposure to that of other schools, to become introverted in their training and outlook.

Under such conditions, kata came to assume an enlarged role in the teaching and learning process. For new generations of first students and then teachers who had never known combat, pattern practice became their only exposure to martial skills. As instructors grew further and further away from battlefield and dueling experience, and as evaluation of student progress came to be based on performance in pattern practice alone, it became increasingly difficult to determine whether or not students actually understood the kata they were performing. In some schools, skill in pattern practice became an end in and of itself. Kata grew showier and more stylized, while trainees danced their way through them with little attempt to internalize anything but the outward form.

By the end of the seventeenth century, Ogyu Sorai and other self-styled experts on proper samurai behavior were already mourning the decline of the bugei and martial training. The warrior arts of ages past, they lamented, had degenerated into "flowery swordplay" (*kaho kenpo*) and gamesmanship. In the words of Fujita Toko, an early nineteenth century commentator:

> Tests of arms with live blades ceased to be conducted. When this happened, the various houses founded their own schools and practiced only within their own ryuha. Thus… [training] came to be like children's play wherein one stud-

---

[13] Although government prohibitions on inter-school contests did not eliminate the practice completely, they did provide a convenient excuse for any would-be instructor who wished to avoid such matches. A similar phenomenon appears to have occurred in the late twentieth century: the headmaster of one ryuha once commented to me that in the early 1960s, when taryu jiai were a common practice, there were only a handful of schools active in any public forum. Since the late '60s, when stricter Japanese government enforcement of its dueling laws put an end to taryu jiai, the number of ryuha participating in demonstrations and the like has waxed appreciably (personal conversation with Dr. Seki Humitake, nineteenth generation *shihanke*, Kashima-Shinryu, August 14, 1992).

ied only kata; the arts of sword and spear could not but decline. (quoted in Ishioka, Wakada, and Kato 20)

It should be emphasized, however, that the potential problems inherent in pattern practice are just that: *potential* problems, not *inevitable* ones. Not all ryuha lapsed into kaho kenpo during the middle Tokugawa period. Some were able to keep their kata alive, practical, and in touch with their roots, their kabala in the hands of men who had genuinely mastered it.[14] In this context Sorai seems to have drawn a distinction between the Toda-ryu and the Shinto-ryu on the one hand, and the Yagyu Shinkage-ryu and the Itto-ryu on the other.[15] Nevertheless, a good many ryuha gradually reified methods and conventions they did not fully understand, and fossilized kata, passing on only the outward forms without fully comprehending the principles behind them. This danger may have been particularly acute for schools, such as the Yagyu Shinkage-ryu, in which the headship was restricted to a single family, as it was difficult to guarantee that each generation would produce a son equal to his ancestors in talent and diligence. In any event, by the end of the seventeenth century, the shortcomings of pattern practice were provoking both commentary and responses.

In the early 1700s several sword schools in Edo began experimenting with protective gear to allow their students to spar with one another at full speed and power without injury.[16] This touched off a debate that continues to this day.

---

[14] This is attested to by the undefeated records, in dozens of taryu jiai, of Kunii Zen'ya and Seki Humitake, two recent headmasters of the Kashima-Shinryu, a school that continues to train only through pattern practice.

[15] See the passage quoted in Ishioka, Wakada, and Kato (21).

[16] Kamiizumi Ise-no-Kami Nobutsuna is believed to have been the first famous swordsman to adopt the bamboo practice sword (*fukuro shinai* or *hikihada shinai*) in the late sixteenth century. Naganuma Shirozaemon Kunisato, of the Jikishinkage-ryu, is usually credited with introducing head and wrist protection in the 1710s.

Proponents of sparring and the competitions that developed concomitantly argued that pattern practice alone cannot develop the seriousness of purpose, the courage, decisiveness, aggressiveness, and forbearance vital to true mastery of combat. Such skills can be fostered only by contesting with an equally serious opponent, not by dancing through kata. Pattern practice, moreover, forces students to pull their blows and slow them down, so they never develop their speed and striking power. Competition, it was argued, is also needed to teach students how to read and respond to an opponent who is actually trying to strike them.

Kata purists, on the other hand, retorted that competitive sparring does *not* produce the same state of mind as real combat and is not, therefore, any more realistic a method of training than pattern practice. Sparring also inevitably requires rules and modifications of equipment that move trainees even further away from the conditions of duels and/or the battlefield. Moreover, sparring distracts students from the mastery of the kata and encourages them to develop their own moves and techniques, before they have fully absorbed those of the ryuha.

The controversy persists today, with little foreseeable prospect of resolution.[17] It is important for our purposes here to note that it represents a divergence in philosophy that transcends the label of traditionalists versus reformers sometimes applied to it. In the first place, the conflict is nearly three hundred years old, and the "traditionalist" position only antedates the "reformist" one by a few decades. In the second, advocates of sparring maintain that their methodology is actually closer to that employed in Sengoku and early Tokugawa times than is kata-only training. And in the third place, modern cognate martial arts schools — the true reformists — are divided over this issue: judo relies exclusively on sparring to evaluate students, while aikido tests only by means of kata, and kendo uses a combination of kata and sparring in its examinations. In any event, one must be careful not to make

---

[17] For recent discussions of this issue, see Nakabayashi (1988), Yoshitani (114-29), Tomiki (5-9, 13-25, 52-101), or Iwai (58-67, 88-107).

too much of the quarrels surrounding pattern practice. For the disagreements are disputes of degree, not essence. All of the traditional ryuha that survive today utilize kata as their central form of training. None has abandoned it or subordinated it to other teaching techniques.

Kata, then, are a key component of traditional Japanese martial art. They are kabala in motion, dynamic compendiums of the essential principles of the various schools. Pattern practice is the core of transmission in the traditional ryuha, the fundamental means for teaching and learning that body of knowledge that constitutes the school. Mastery of a ryuha's secrets is a supra-rational process wherein one is first molded by, then freed from, and finally freed *by* the framework of the ryuha's kata.

References

Dore, R. 1965. *Education in Tokugawa Japan*. Berkeley, CA: UC Press.

Draeger, D.F. 1973. *Classical Budo*. The Martial Arts and Ways of Japan, 2. New York & Tokyo: Weatherhill.

Eno, R. 1990. *The Confucian Creation of Heaven: Philosophy and the Defense of Ritual Mastery*. Albany, NY: State University of New York Press.

Fung, Y. 1948. *A Short History of Chinese Philosophy*. New York: The Free Press.

Hori, G.V.S. 1994. Teaching and Learning in the Rinzai Zen Monastery. *Journal of Japanese Studies* 20, no. 1: 5-35.

Imamura Y., ed. 1982. *Nihon Budo Taikei.* 10 vols. Tokyo: Dohosha Shuppan.

Inagaki M. 1982. *Kengo no Meishobu 100 Wa.* Tokyo: Tatsukaze Shobo.

Ishioka H., Wakada K., and Kato H. 1980. *Nihon no Kobujutsu.* Tokyo: Shinjinbutsu Oraisha.

Iwai T. 1991. *Kobujutsu Tankyu.* Tokyo: Airyudo.

Kobe S. 1984. *Nihon Kengodan.* Tokyo: Mainichi Shinbunsha.

Kurogi T. 1967. Budo Ryuha No Seiritsu to Shugendo. *Saga-dai Kyoiku Gakubu Kenkyu Ronbunshu* 15: 159-93.

Nakabayashi S. 1982. Kendo Shi. In *Nihon Budo Taikei*, edited by Imamura Y., vol. 10. Tokyo: Dohosha Shuppan.

————. 1988. Kenjutsu Keiko no Ikkosai. In *Budo Ronko.* Ibaraki: Nakabayashi Shinji Sensei Isakushu Kangyokai.

Okada K. 1984. *Kengo Shidan.* Tokyo: Shinjinbutsu Oraisha.

Seki H. 1976. *Nihon Budo no Engen: Kashima-Shinryu.* Tokyo: Kyorin Shoin.

Slawson, D. 1987. *Secret Teachings in the Art of Japanese Gardens: Design Principles and Aesthetic Values.* Tokyo: Kodansha International.

Sugawara, M. 1985. *Lives of Master Swordsmen.* Tokyo: The East.

Suzuki, D.T. 1959. *Zen and Japanese Culture.* Princeton, NJ: Princeton University Press.

Tomiki K. 1991. *Budo Ron*. Tokyo: Daishukan Shoten.

Tominaga K. 1971. *Kendo Gohyakunen-shi*. Tokyo: Hyakusen Shobo.

Ukai, N. 1994. The Kumon Approach to Teaching and Learning. *Journal of Japanese Studies* 20, no. 1: 87-113.

Watanabe I., ed. 1979. *Budo no Meicho*. Tokyo: Tokyo Kopii Shuppanbu.

Watatani K. 1971. *Nihon Kengo 100 Sen*. Tokyo: Akita Shoten.

Yoshitani O. 1988. Kenjutsu Kata no Kozo to Kino ni Kansuru Kenkyu. In *Nihon Budogaku Kenkyu*, edited by Watanabe Ichiro Kyoju Taikan Kinenkai. Tokyo: Shimazu Shobo.

Nishioka Tsuneo began his training in Shinto Muso-ryu in 1938 under Shimizu Takaji, from whom he received menkyo kaiden, a license of complete transmission. He also holds the teaching license and grade of hanshi hachidan, awarded by the All-Japan Kendo Federation. He is the author of several books on the martial arts and heads the Seiryukai, a group devoted to preserving the teachings of Shimizu Sensei.

Uchidachi and Shidachi

Nishioka Tsuneo

The following text has as its core a translation of a chapter in Nishioka Tsuneo's book *Budo-teki na Mono no Kangaekata: Shu, Ha, Ri* (*Budo Way of Thinking: Shu, Ha, Ri*). Direct translations from the Japanese are frequently problematic because of the ambiguity inherent in the traditional Japanese style of essay writing. In order to clarify the author's ideas and best present his thoughts in English, we have supplemented the original text with a series of personal conversations.[1] The result thus intentionally suggests the flavor of teachings passed down from master to disciple.

Please note that in this essay, the suffixes -*do* (way) and -*jutsu* (skill or technique) are used in the Japanese fashion — that is to say, without making a precise distinction between them. The author believes that they are not two distinct entities, but different facets of a single whole. It is this whole to which he refers, sometimes as budo, sometimes as bujutsu. In places he uses terminology typical of a classical art, while at other times he uses terms usually applied when discussing modern budo. His comments are intended to cover both.

The essay begins with reference to the Japanese concept of *rei*. This word presents unique difficulties in translation. Although rei translates as etiquette, decorum, propriety, politeness, or courtesy, none of these terms are quite equivalent to the Japanese, so in this essay we will not provide an English substitute. Think of it as the proper essence or quality of relationships between individuals.   – *Diane Skoss*

---

[1] Special thanks to Phil Relnick, Larry Bieri, Meik Skoss, Joe Cieslik, Dave Lowry, Roger and Miho Lloyd, Dan Soares, Derek Steel, and Steve Duncan. The original translation is by Yoko Sato; Diane Skoss provided the footnotes and introduction. *Uchidachi*, 打太刀, "striking sword"; *shidachi*, 仕太刀, "doing sword."

The heart of bujutsu is *rei*. The responsibility of a teacher is to communicate this to students. If this communication fails, students can develop incorrect attitudes and the true meaning of training is lost. Unfortunately, there is a great deal of abuse of power in Japanese budo today. In my opinion few teachers are teaching the principles of budo correctly. Rei in budo has become very artificial, resembling the old-style Japanese military hierarchy. The true meaning of rei is no longer expressed. We seem to be preserving only the worst parts of Japanese traditions and culture, and we need to consider ways to change this situation.

Bujutsu leads to rei. The instructor ideally behaves as an exemplar to lead students toward something higher. Rei is an expression of humility towards that higher existence. But some people, as they develop their skills and achieve higher rank, dismiss what they ought to have learned about rei. Those who fail to work as diligently to improve the spirit as they do to improve their techniques are likely to forget the proper humility of true rei. They are apt to become overconfident, proud, and patronizing. Spiritual development and technical development are entirely different things and there is not necessarily any relationship between them.

Training in jojutsu, for example, has a wonderful quality because it can result in both sorts of development; spiritual growth leads to technical growth and vice versa. Development is not merely a matter of technique. However, if physical techniques are taught improperly or superficially, students will become confused. There will be even greater misunderstanding if the focus is only on the process of polishing techniques. We must never lose sight of the intent to "correct and improve the spirit." The only way to ensure this is to study under a master teacher.

In general, people misunderstand what a master teacher is. They can become confused, equating the idea of a master with that of an instructor or a senior. Unfortunately, as one's skill level increases, so, often, does the size of one's ego. Too frequently, younger people who are of high rank or who have received a license or scroll assume that they are qualified to be a teacher just because they have instructor certification, own a dojo, or have students. It is a grave error to believe that a person is a master teacher just because of a high rank or license.

Once, my teacher, Shimizu Takaji Sensei (1896-1978), told me not to copy the jo practiced by his junior fellow student Otofuji Ichizo Sensei. Unless one carefully reflects on what Shimizu Sensei really meant, this statement can be easily misunderstood. He knew that there were some differences between his way of using *jo* and *tachi*, and the way in which Otofuji Sensei used these weapons. Even in *kata bujutsu*,[2] it is very natural for there to be differences in the form. That's because different people have different levels of technical understanding and different mindsets. This leads them to make movements in slightly different ways and they pass on these individual characteristics in their teaching. Shimizu Sensei was afraid that young students would notice these differences, get confused or suspicious, and think that one way or the other was wrong. He seemed to have been concerned about the inevitable errors that result when a student is unable or unwilling to follow just one teacher. He urged me to follow a single teacher, to the greatest extent possible, and to avoid confusing myself unnecessarily by looking around at other teachers.

Having more than one teacher can create serious problems in your training. On the other hand, insisting that students blindly "follow one and only one teacher" can result in separatist cliques and prevent students of different teachers from being able to practice together. This distasteful situation still occurs in the Japanese martial arts world. The only solution is to wait for the spiritual growth of both the teacher and

---

[2] This term is Japanese shorthand for old-style martial arts that are practiced using *kata* (see Karl Friday's "Kabala in Motion," page 151, for a complete discussion of the kata training method) as the primary teaching tool. Unlike karate kata, in which moves are practiced solo, kata bujutsu consists of kata practiced in pairs, one attacking (shidachi) and one receiving (uchidachi). This can be done with the same weapons (i.e. tachi versus tachi) or different ones (jo versus tachi, *naginata* versus *kusarigama*, etc.). The classical Japanese arts tend to focus almost exclusively on kata-style training, while many of the modern budo incorporate kata as only one component of a larger curriculum.

*Quintin Chambers (left) demonstrating the chudan technique kengomi.
Nishioka Tsuneo is acting as uchidachi. Hawaii 1995.*

the disciple; then students can train under a single teacher and still benefit from interacting with students from other groups.

This is why an understanding of rei is so essential to the process of spiritual growth in bujutsu. One of the most profound expressions of rei lies in the interaction between *uchidachi*, the one who receives the technique, and *shidachi*, the one who does the technique. Unfortunately, even teachers often misunderstand the subtleties of uchidachi and shidachi in *kata* training. They fail to pass on to their students the difference in intent inherent in these two roles. Particularly in the classical traditions, the roles of uchidachi and shidachi are quite distinctive. Each has its own unique psychological viewpoint. It is essential that this distinct quality always be maintained. I believe that the difference in these two roles is the defining characteristic of kata training. Recently, I've come to the realization that it is not even worth training unless both partners properly understand this.

When an outsider watches kata, it appears that uchidachi loses and shidachi wins. This is intentional. But there's much more to it than that. Uchidachi must have the spirit of a nurturing parent. Uchidachi leads shidachi by providing a true attack; this allows shidachi to learn correct body displacement, combative distancing, proper spirit, and the perception of opportunity. A humble spirit is as necessary as correct technique for uchidachi. Deceit, arrogance, and a patronizing attitude must never be allowed in practice. *Uchidachi's mission is vital.* In the past, this role was only performed by senior practitioners who were capable of performing accurate technique and who possessed the right spirit and understanding of the role. Uchidachi must provide an example of clean, precise cutting lines and correct targeting, and must also convey focused intensity and an air of authority.

If uchidachi is the parent or teacher, then shidachi is the child or disciple. The goal is to acquire the skills presented by uchidachi's technique. Unfortunately, students often act as though they want to test their skills against those of the higher-ranked uchidachi. They consider this competition to be their practice. In fact, this leads to neither better technique, nor greater spiritual development, because the correct relationship between uchidachi and shidachi has been obscured. It is the repetition of the techniques in this parent/child or senior/junior relationship that allows for the growth of the spirit through the practice of technique.

The roles of uchidachi as senior and shidachi as junior are preserved regardless of the actual respective experience levels of the pair. Kata must be practiced so that trainees learn both to give and to receive. This is what makes technical improvement and spiritual development possible. Unfortunately, in jo practice, people sometimes think that they practice both roles merely to memorize the sequential movements of the two different weapons, tachi and jo. There are even some instructors who teach that the aim of Shinto Muso-ryu jojutsu is to learn how to defeat a sword with a stick. This is an error. If it continues, kata bujutsu may die out, because both the technique and the spirit of uchidachi will not improve.

These days there are fewer people who can perform the role of uchidachi correctly. I believe that bujutsu evolved into budo only by maintaining the idea of uchidachi and shidachi. This idea is a fundamental characteristic of the classical bujutsu. Although the Japanese arts, such as kenjutsu, iaijutsu, and jojutsu, have been transformed from "jutsu" into "do," if the proper roles in training are not preserved, the "do" arts will veer off in the wrong direction. Obviously, there is a difference between attempting to preserve the proper distinction between uchidachi and shidachi yet not achieving perfection, and a complete lack of effort or understanding about the distinction. The existence of the intent or the quality of the intent is manifested in daily practice and actions. Those who have the eyes and experience to see can tell the difference.

However, my concern is that these days fewer people understand this concept. In the future there will be fewer still. People seem no longer to recognize that the existence of uchidachi and shidachi is the essence of budo training.

All things considered, I am convinced that the most important things I have learned from Shinto Muso-ryu and Shimizu Takaji Sensei are the roles of uchidachi and shidachi in kata. There is no way to transmit the kata of the Japanese classical traditions without a proper understanding of this spirit of giving and receiving. It is not right for seniors in the uchidachi role to mistreat, bully, or torment their juniors. On the contrary, their job is to guide and educate. In the same sense, it is also terrible to see shidachi assume an attitude that is essentially patricidal, and attempt to destroy the uchidachi. I can only say that such a spirit should never exist.

Shimizu Sensei always said, "You must train with me" [i.e. directly with your own teacher]. He constantly took the role of uchidachi. Even with beginners, he never relaxed his attention. He was always serious with everyone. He was never arrogant and never lorded it over another person. I believe that this attitude is the most important teaching of kata bujutsu, and Shimizu Sensei's training was a wonderful example. This spirit is difficult to nurture, not only in jojutsu but in other situations as well. It is entirely different from a senior student or teacher

Shimizu Yuji (right) performing the final movement (osame) of a jojutsu kata while Nishioka Tsuneo (as uchidachi) maintains zanshin. Internationl Jodo Federation gathering, Hawaii 1994.

showing off his skills to his juniors by treating them with arrogance and condescension. It is so easy to become trapped in a cycle of interaction that causes shidachi to react by attempting to compete with uchidachi. The guidance of a master teacher is absolutely essential to avoid this situation.

Uchidachi teaches shidachi by sacrificing himself, training as if he were going to be killed at any moment; this self-sacrifice embodies the spirit of teachers and parents. Kata training is of no use without understanding this. It is this spirit that allows shidachi to grow and polish his or her own spirit. Kata bujutsu teaches neither victory nor defeat, but rather how to nurture others and pull them to a higher level. That is budo.

I earnestly hope that everyone, particularly those who practice jojutsu, remember this axiom: "Do not be jubilant in victory; do not become servile in defeat. Lose with dignity." This is the spirit we must emulate.

INDEX

A

agura (cross-seated position)
    See sitting positions, *agura*
aikido   xi, 166
aikuchi (small dagger)
    See weapons, *aikuchi*
aiuchi (mutual strike)   109
Aizu domain   94
Akiyama Shirobei Yoshitoki (Yoshin-ryu
    founder)   61
Amdur, Ellis   xi, 113 - 115, 147
Analects, Confucian
    See Confucian *Analects*
Araki-ryu gunyo kogusoku   113
armor (*yoroi, katchu*)   76
    in training   101 - 102, 165
    opponents in   129
    techniques for use when wearing
    See *katchu bujutsu*
Armstrong, Hunter B.   112, 115 - 117,
    126, 144, 147 - 148
Asayama Ichiden-ryu heiho   163
ashigaru (foot soldiers)
    See *bushi*
Ashikaga Yoshiaki (1537-1597)   40
Ashikaga Yoshiteru (1536-1565)   39
Azuchi-Momoyama period (1568-1600)
    38

B

bakufu
    See shogunate
battlefield   31, 54, 124, 166
    experience on   53, 164
    gallantry (*tegara*)   53
    modern   101, 105

    See also combat, training for;
        katchu bujutsu; strategy and
        tactics
battoiai
    See Takenouchi-ryu
battojutsu (sword-drawing techniques)
    See *iaijutsu*
    Shojitsu Kenri Kataichi-ryu   76
bo (staff)
    See weapons, *bo*
bojutsu (staff techniques)
    Kiraku-ryu   64
    Takenouchi-ryu   73 - 74
    Tatsumi-ryu   70
    Tenshin Shoden Katori Shinto-ryu
        67 - 68
    Toda-ha Buko-ryu   64 - 65
    Yoshin-ryu   61
bokken (wooden sword)
    See training weapons, *bokken*
bokuto (wooden sword)
    See training weapons, *bokuto*
boxing and karate   89 - 90, 102
breath control (*kokyu*)   72, 135
Buddha   28
Buddhism, esoteric
    See *mikkyo*
Buddhism, Zen
    See Zen
budo (martial way)   37, 101 - 102, 171,
    173, 176 - 177
Budo Shoshinshu   55
bugei (martial arts)   152 - 157, 161,
    163 - 164, 171
bujutsu (martial arts/techniques)   13 -
    15, 89, 102, 104, 171, 174, 176
buke (warrior family)   120

Index 181

Index   183

Index

Koryu Online:
The Internet Resource
of the Classical Martial Arts
http://www.koryubooks.com/

A unique compendium of photographs, essays, excerpts, book reviews, and more. Visit soon and take advantage of the wealth of free information we have collected, and keep up-to-date on the latest Koryu Books publications. If you'd like to read more quality books like this one, check out our special online bookstore, where you can read detailed reviews of our carefully selected recommendations, then order any title for immediate shipment. Your satisfaction with your purchase is 100% guaranteed or your money will be cheerfully refunded.